TABLE OF CONTENTS

Chemical Reactions - Continued

Carboxylic acids

Carboxylic acids are compounds formed when a carboxyl group (CO_2H) bonds to a hydrocarbon unit such as an alkane or alkene. Formic, acetic, and stearic acids are common carboxylic acids. In decarboxylation of these compounds, a substitution reaction, the carboxyl group is replaced by a hydrogen atom. These reactions are important in biological processes. These acids may also be converted to anhydrides (compounds without water) by reactions, usually at high temperature, which break the bonds in the carboxyl group and produce H_2O. Cleaving the C=O bond and removing the OH group from the carboxyl results in an acyl with double or triple bonds between the C and remaining O. These groups react quickly with halides to form compounds such as acyl chloride (OCCl).

$$:O:$$
$$\sigma$$
$$-C-O-$$
$$H$$

Benzenes

Benzene (C_6H_6) is an important cyclic organic compound. The electrons of its C atoms are delocalized resulting in combinations of single and double bonds, a structure which gives benzenes unusual stability. Compounds with strong, usually pleasant odors are often attached to benzene parents, so early chemists named these compounds aromatic compounds. Many benzene compounds have no odor, however. Common reactions include the following:

Aromatic electrophilic substitution is the most important class of reactions associated with benzene. In these reactions an H atom of the benzene is replaced by an electrophile which can be an atom or, more often, a molecule or functional group. This class contains subclasses of reactions such as halogenation (benzene + a halogen), nitration (benzene + a nitrate), sulfonation (benzene + a sulfate), alkylation and acylation.

- 4 -

Amines and amides

Amines ($R—NH_2$) are a functional group containing nitrogen which form compounds vital to biological processes. They from when a hydrogen from an ammonia molecule (NH_3) is replaced by an organic compound. They can be primary, secondary, or tertiary amines, depending on how many atoms are bonded to the N atom. Amines react with acyl chlorides ($Cl—C=O$) and acid anhydrides in nucleophilic substitution, producing amides. They neutralize carboxylic acid in an acid-base reaction to produce ammonium carboxylate. Tertiary amines react with strong halogen acids to form ammonium salts. Amides ($O=C—N$) are another functional group; the most important of their reactions is hydrolysis in which the addition of water severs the C—N bond to create amine and carboxylic acid.

Esters

Esters ($O=C—O$) are a functional group often derived from carboxylic acids from which a H atom has been removed. This process is usually a condensation reaction in which two hydrogen-containing groups or compounds react, joining their H and releasing it as water product. Such condensation reactions that produce an ester are called esterification reactions. The most important class of reactions associated with esters is hydrolysis, a reaction in which the ester is broken down by water to yield an alcohol and a carboxylic acid or salt. Hydrolysis of esters may be catalyzed by acid or a base; if the catalyst is a base, the process if called saponification. Esters may also form amides through a reaction with primary or secondary amines at high temperatures.

Ethers

Ethers are a functional group containing an O atom bonded to two alkyl groups. "Ethers" is also the name of the class of chemicals containing an ether group. They are somewhat soluble in water because the O bonds readily with H, and they have a relatively low boiling point. Ethers can be derived from the dehydration of alcohols through heat and a hydrogen-rich catalyst. Nucleophilic displacement of alkyl halides also yields ethers. Ethers are not very reactive in the pure state, but their substituents groups can be highly combustible, as with diethyl ether. Hydrolysis breaks ethers down, but only under drastic conditions such as boiling in the presence of strong halogen acids. Ethers form explosive peroxides in reactions with adjacent CH groups.

Acyl halides

An acyl halide is a compound derived from either a hydrogen acid or a carboxylic acid in which a hydroxyl group (–OH) has been replaced by a halogen. A double bond forms between C and O with two single bonds joining the C with the halogen atom and a root molecule. Acyl halides are synthetic molecules and are most often used as intermediates in reactions to form other compounds. In hydrolysis reactions, they form carboxylic acid and a hydrogen halide. They are also useful in forming esters through a substitution reaction with alcohol, and amides by reacting with amines. They also react with benzene (aromatic) rings to form an aromatic ketone using a strong acid catalyst. Acyl halides are quite reactive and somewhat toxic.

Selective organic reactions

- Reactions in which a certain type of product is preferred though various isomers are equally possible are called selective reactions. A prefix before selective identifies the type of isomer predominately formed in such selective reactions. Enantioselectivity refers to the tendency of a reaction to form a specific enantiomer (nonsuperimposable stereoisomer).
- Regioselectivity is the same principle applied to "regions" of the molecule; some reactions produce more compounds with a specific orientation of appended groups than isomers with different orientations.
- Diastereomers are isomers which are not mirror images of each other and can exhibit different properties and reactivity. Diastereoselectivity describes reactions

in which one stereoisomer is preferred over another as product; the reaction produces more of the favored variety.

Wöhler synthesis

The Wöhler synthesis is an important reaction in the study of organic chemistry. Friedrich Wöhler synthesized urea, an organic compound, from inorganic elements (ammonium cyanate) in 1828, providing a key to modern study of organic chemistry. Prior to Wöhler, chemists believed that organic compounds could not be synthesized and were animated by something called the "living force."

Metabolic pathways

Metabolism refers to an organization's ability through chemical reactions to produce and/or consume energy. Metabolic pathways are complex series of reactions in living cells which enable those biological processes. The pathways are highly complex, but well ordered and predictable, consisting of a series of chemical reactions designed either for catabolism—the breakdown of biomolecules, usually to produce energy, or anabolism—the synthesis of biomolecules. Photosysnthesis is a widely known metabolic pathway which allows green plants to use energy from sunlight, water, and nutrients to produce the energy they need to live and grow. The processes commonly referred to as digestion, by which the human body extracts energy from food, is a series of enormous metabolic pathways. Because the chemical reactions involved are often not species-specific, understanding a metabolic pathway on a molecular and chemical level applies to other organisms that use the same process.

Biochemistry

- Carbohydrates, also called sugars, starch, and cellulose, are complex organic molecules used as sources of energy by many life forms. They contain only C, H, and

- 7 -

O, and occur in many sizes from simple forms, called monosaccharides, to complex polysaccharides.

- Lipids are also called fats in their solid state and oils in their liquid state. They can be broken down through catalyzed reactions and separated from their constituent fatty acids. They are insoluble in water and are vital parts of living cells.
- Proteins are complex molecules formed of long chains of peptides (polypeptides) and are fundamental to many living functions, including cell construction. Collagens, elastins, keratins, and antibodies are common proteins.
- Peptides are compounds of two or more linked amino acids.
- Enzymes are specialized compounds acting as catalysts for reactions necessary for life.

Carbohydrates:

Carbohydrates are important organic molecules containing carbon, hydrogen, and oxygen; they are the primary source of energy for most living organisms. Carbohydrate digestion is the result of several fundamental metabolic pathways associated with them, each process involving a great many subsidiary reactions. The formation of glucose from carbohydrates is one important pathway. Glucose ($C_6H_{12}O_6$) is one of several monosaccharides produced from carbohydrates by chemical reactions. Glucose molecules then enter another metabolic pathway called glycolysis in which they are broken down into pyruvate ($C_3H_4O_3$), which in turn begins another series of cascading reactions which lead to usable energy. The citric acid cycle is another important metabolic pathway in the digestion of carbohydrates.

Lipids:

Lipids are biomolecules that are insoluble in water but soluble in other nonpolar solvents. They are responsible for the waxy or greasy nature of substances found in plants and animals. Saponification is a process used to further distinguish classes of lipids; it is the process by which esters are hydrolyzed in base solution to yield glycerol and the salts of fatty acids. If lipids do not contain esters, they are nonsaponifiable and are classified accordingly. Hydrolysis is another important reaction for lipids. In the presence of water

Copyright © Mometrix Media. You have been licensed one copy of this document for personal use only. Any other reproduction or redistribution is strictly prohibited. All rights reserved.

and an acid catalyst, lipids break down into glycerol and fatty acids. Hydrogenation is the process of converting C=H double bonds to C—H single bonds resulting in increased saturation of the hydrocarbon and a correspondingly higher melting point.

Proteins:

Proteins can also be metabolized for use as a source of energy, but this is merely one catabolic pathway associated with them. Because proteins are constructed of long chains of amino acids, reactions early in the process are of particular interest. One is the oxidation of cysteine, a sulfur-containing amino acid. Two cysteine molecules combine with oxygen and fuse to form a S—S disulfide bond, creating one molecule of cystine. This reaction is important in determining the unique structure of some proteins. Peptides are groups of two or more linked amino acids. Peptide formation occurs during protein synthesis when a carboxyl group reacts with an amine of a second amino acid to release water and form an amide bond which links the two amino acids into a peptide. The amide bond is called a peptide bond; many such reactions can produce long chains (polypeptides) that eventually become proteins.

Protein hydrolysis and denaturation:

Protein hydrolysis is one of the processes within the metabolic pathway that produces energy for use by living cells. Proteins may be hydrolyzed by acids or bases or by water due to its highly polar molecules. Long protein chains are broken into smaller peptides, and, with increased time, temperature, or acidity/basicity, the peptides can be reduced to individual amino acids. Hydrolysis reactions in digestion are catalyzed by enzymes present in animals' digestive systems. Denaturation is the process by which the orderly structure of natural proteins is broken through exposure to conditions such as high temperatures and certain compounds. The protein's folds and helical structures straighten and twist into random forms, making the protein inactive. Denaturation of toxic proteins explains why boiling water to kill bacteria makes it safe to drink—the bacteria no longer produce harmful proteins and the present proteins become denatured.

Enzymes:

Some of the most important functions associated with enzymes regulate their activity. Enzymes can exist in an inactive or preactive state called zymogens or proenzymes. They are stored until needed by a cell for a specific reaction and are then released and activated to become active enzymes. They are activated by breaking one or more peptide bonds on the enzyme through hydrolysis reactions. Enzyme activity is also regulated by substances called modulators which bond to the enzyme and change its three dimensional orientation, rendering it temporarily inactive. Modulators can be either activators, which increase the enzyme's activity, or inhibitors, which decrease it. Some substances act as uncontrollable, irreversible inhibitors and are thus highly toxic. Cyanide and other heavy metals are deadly because of their inhibitory functions. Enzyme inhibition is a process in which products at the end of reactions inhibit earlier reaction steps, effectively regulating the concentration of target compounds.

Enzymes are catalysts in metabolic pathways and play roles in very large numbers of reactions; all of them are globular proteins and catalyze reactions involving other proteins, making them of fundamental importance in complex bioprocesses. Most enzymes are highly selective, catalyzing only specific reactions when the reactants come into contact with the reactive site of the much larger enzyme molecule. For instance, the enzyme urease is a catalyst in only one reaction: the hydroloysis of urea. By contrast, other catalysts, such as strong acids or bases, catalyze they hydrolysis of any amide. Enzymes are complex proteins that are highly catalytic, increasing the rate of some reactions by as much as 10^{20} times. Enzymes are named systematically with a set of conventions much like IUPAC nomenclature. These conventions specify the reactant and functional group acted upon and the type of reaction catalyzed. A suffix –ase indicates the named compound is an enzyme.

Nucleic acids

Nucleic acids are polymers composed of many smaller nucleotides which can be further broken down to phosphoric acid, organic bases, amines, and deoxyribose or ribose. The nucleotides link to form the polymers in an alternating sequence of phosphate units and sugar units. A nucleic acid containing deoxyribose as its sugar is deoxyribonucleic acid, or DNA. If ribose is the sugar, the compound is ribonucleic acid, or RNA. Nucleic acids are important substances in biochemistry; DNA is the fundamental constituent of genes carrying hereditary information and occurs in a complex molecular arrangement known as the double helix. RNA is a compound essential to the proper formation and utilization of proteins within cells and is found in several varieties including the most common tRNA (transfer RNA) mRNA (messenger RNA).

Codons:

Codons are long molecules formed of nucleotides and found in mRNA. Each codon is specific to the protein in whose synthesis it plays a lead role, so each one has unique properties such as molecular weight. Codons are long because they contain three nucleotides for each amino acid required by their target protein. They are attached to ribosomes, which can move through several codons of the mRNA during protein synthesis. The ribosome chemically activates the appropriate codon to form amino acids in proper sequence for the necessary protein. It is a codon which eventually signals the completion of the protein and the separation of the peptide chain from the ribosome.

Protein synthesis

One of the most fundamental processes for life, protein synthesis is a complex series of reactions involving large compounds. The synthesis occurs at the surface of ribosomal RNA (rRNA) particles suspended in the cytoplasm of cells. Amino acids bonded to transfer RNA (tRNA) are brought to the sites and the translation of codons into a sequence of amino acids begins if the required compounds are present. If all requirements are met, a series of enzyme-catalyzed steps begins to form long peptide chains. The process begins with the initiation step and concludes with termination, at which point the protein is separated from the rRNA. Most proteins are not yet in the form needed by the cell and are modified by more complex reactions to produce the needed protein.

The Krebs cycle

Also known as the citric acid cycle, the Krebs cycle is an important metabolic pathway in the series of pathways by which large molecules are broken down into energy for use by living organisms. It was named for its discoverer, Hans Adolf Krebs, who described the pathway in 1937. The cycle is the their pathway in the metabolism of sugars. After a person eats a meal, for example, the food particles are converted to glucose and/or glycerol; they then undergo another pathway which further reduces the glucose/glycerol molecules to pyruvate, and then yet further to acetyl coenzyme A. That substance then enters the Krebs cycle where a complex series of reactions produce ATP (adenosine triphosphate) and NAD (nicotinamide adenine dinucleotide), and NADP (nicotinamide adenine dinucleotide phosphate). A number of other pathways feed into the cycle at various points, providing necessary inputs and outputs for it and for other pathways.

Components:
The citric acid (or Krebs) cycle takes place within the mitochondria of cells. It follows glycolysis and oxidative decarboxylation in the string of metabolic pathways through which sugars are converted to forms of energy usable by cells. It involves two rotations, or turns through the cycle and begins when a molecule of acetyl coenzyme A (acetyl-CoA) Acetyl-CoA forms citrate (a carboxylic acid also called citric acid) by reacting with a four-carbon carboxylate. A series of reactions converts the citrate back to a four-carbon carboxylate, releasing CO_2 in the process and producing 1 ATP, 3 NADH, and 3 FADH. Because the input of pyruvic acid involves two molecules, the cycle "turns" again doubling the products to 2 ATP, 6 NADH, and 6 FADH. Water and 4 CO_2 are expelled as by-products.

Environmental issues

The non-human world:
The value of the non-human world to society is the heart of the impact of science on the environment. The increasing power of our technology and our population explosion

increase our capacity to stress ecosystems. This capacity has global as well as local effects. Issues such as global warming, radioactive fallout and its residual danger, are examples of global effects of technology. The non-human world has value to us in two major ways:

1. Instrumental Value - The non-human world is valued in terms of its usefulness to humans and society. Many decisions, both political and economic, are made based on the instrumental value of the non-human world.

2. Intrinsic Value - The non-human world is valued for itself, regardless of its usefulness to humans. This may lead to an arbitrary assignment of value based on any number of criteria. For example, living organisms may have a higher intrinsic value than inanimate matter. They may be assigned value based on their complexity or capacities.

Environmental debate:

The two extremes of the environmental debate serve to illustrate the diversity of thought in this area.

1. The Technocratic Cornucopianism - This position claims there is no shortage of resources on earth. Humans must develop more sophisticated technologies to harvest these resources. Earth provides an infinite well of resources for those clever and industrious enough to tap them.

2. The Deep Ecology Movement - The key themes in this view are the stressing of the principles of diversity and symbiosis. It argues for a biocentric approach, insisting on the equality of all species. This position sees man as a part of the biosphere, rather than apart and distinct from the world. It posits a "relational, total-field image".

Between these two extremes is the mainstream of environmental concern, and the issues that face society in light of our increasing technological power.

Formulating an environmental policy:

Many principles are used in planning environmental policy:

1. Free-market Economics - In this principle the non-human world has no intrinsic value and decisions are made solely on economic concerns. The weakness of this policy is that many natural resources are not owned (the Oceans) and have no financial values.

1. 2 .The Polluter Pays Policy - States the environment may be exploited for economic gain, but the consumer must return the environment to its original condition. This overlooks the fact that much environmental damage is unseen and permanent.

2. Radical Biocentrism - In this principle, all organisms are equal, and cannot be exploited for another's gain. This is an impractical solution, particularly in underdeveloped countries.

3. Environmental Economics - In this scheme, all factors are weighed and decisions based on the principles of common good for society. This involves giving a value to the environment, a concept while valid, is subject to social, political and economic pressures.

Combinations of these principles (and some additional ones) are used to develop and implement environmental policy.

Environmental ethics

Rainforest conservation:

In evaluating problems such as conservation of the rainforests, it is clear many competing human interests are at work. Some possible solutions to these competing demands are:

1. Research, training, and development about the rainforests and its value.

2. Land reform.

3. Ecosystem conservation in selected habitats.

4. Reforestation to remedy exploitation.

5. Economic controls on timber trade.

6. Consumer pressure in developed countries.

7. Changes in aid, debt relief, and investment policies by first world countries.

8. Debt for nature swaps (conservation of habitats in return for debt forgiveness)

9. Marketing of non-tree products pf the forests.

The decisions and implementation inherent in these ideas is complex and subject to social, economic, and political pressures.

Malaria and DDT:

It is now scientifically possible to eradicate or substantially reduce the scourge of malaria in the world through the use of DDT. Although at first glance this seems an easy decision, there are complicating factors involved.

Countries with endemic malaria are poor and can only afford cheap effective pesticides. DDT fits this description, cost-effective, easy to apply, and with lasting effects. The savings in human suffering would be significant. However, mosquitoes, the cause of malaria, are an important part of the tropical ecosystems, providing an important link in the food chain. Also, DDT is not species-specific and affects a large range of organisms from insects to mammals. This problem raises ethical questions:

1. What value is placed on the lives of the affected people?

2. What values can be assigned to affected ecosystems and the biosphere?

3. How can the needs of the country and ecology be met?

The difficulties of answering these questions and formulating policy are apparent. Environmental ethics is a source of much debate and discussion, and will be for years to come.

Reproductive technology:

The scientific advance of reproductive technology has raised a number of ethical issues. They may be summarized as follows:

1. Artificial insemination separates sexual intercourse from procreation.
2. Donor insemination breaks the link between the genetic parent and the nurturing parent.
3. Confidentiality of participants in gamete donation may be breached.
4. Questions of the moral status of embryos and when life begins are of central importance.
5. The use of medical funding and its distribution among the population are raised.
6. Harm may outweigh benefit in some reproductive technologies.

Clearly these issues touch on sensitive topics in ethics, religion, social policy, medicine, and politics. There are no easy or definitive answers but ample room for discussion, education, and argument.

Basic equations of relative motion

One dimension:

In order to demonstrate how relative motion can be expressed in an equation, let us imagine a scenario in which car A is parked by the side of the road as car B moves down the road in a straight line. Both of these cars are observing car C. If both A and B assess the position of C at any given time, the equation will look like this: $x_{ca} = x_{cb} + x_{ba}$, which just means that the position of c as measured by a is equal to the position of c as measured by b plus the position of b as measured by a. We can make a similar equation for velocity, simply by substituting velocity for position in the above equation.

Two dimensions:

When we begin to consider relative motion in two dimensions rather than just one, we begin to work with vectors rather than scalars. Let us create an example: two observers are measuring the velocity of a moving particle, though the two observers are moving apart from one another at a constant velocity. When this is the case, we say that the two observers inhabit inertial reference frames. If the two observers measure the position of particle p at a givens instant, then we may create the vector equation: $r_{PA} = r_{PB} + r_{BA}$. Once the time derivative is taken, there will be a relation in the measured velocities that can be expressed: $v_{PA} = v_{PB} + v_{BA}$. Taking the time derivative of this equation, we can derive a connection between the two measured accelerations: $a_{PA} = a_{PB}$.

Force

A force is something that gives acceleration to some body. Force is a vector; that is, it has both mass and direction. This can be demonstrated by considering an object placed at the origin of the coordinate plane. If it is pushed along the positive direction of the y-axis, it will move in this direction; if the force acting on it is in the positive direction of the x-axis, it will move in that direction. But if both forces are applied at the same time, then the object will move at an angle to both the x and y axes, an angle determined by the relative amount of force exerted in each direction. In this way, we may see that the resulting force is a vector sum; that is, a net force that has both magnitude and direction.

Normal force:

The word "normal" is used in mathematics to mean perpendicular, and so the force known as normal force should be remembered as the perpendicular force exerted on an object that is resting on some other surface. For instance, if a box is resting on a horizontal surface, we may say that the normal force N is directed upwards through the box (the opposite, downward force is the weight of the box). The magnitude of N can be derived by adjusting the equation used for force, such that: $\sum F_y = N - mg = ma_y$. If $a_y = 0$, then $N = mg$.

Mass

If we apply the same force to two objects of a different size, we will often find that the resulting acceleration is different. The reason for this is that the two objects have a different mass. Mass is typically defined as the quantity of matter in an object, but we may wish to be a bit more specific. For instance, if we were to take an object with a predetermined mass (1 kilogram, say), and attach a spring to it, we can know in advance that in order to give it an acceleration of one meter per second squared, we will need to pull with a force of one Newton. If we then replace the kilogram object with some other random object, and again pull on it with a force of one Newton, then we can find the mass of the object by assuming that the ratio of the masses will be inverse to the ratio of the accelerations. That is: $\frac{m_x}{m_0} = \frac{a_0}{a_x}$. In this way, we may assign masses to other bodies than the standard, one kilogram body.

Weight

Too often, weight is confused with mass. Strictly, weight is the force pulling a body towards the center of a nearby astronomical body. Of course, in the case of most day-to-day operations for human beings, that astronomical body is the earth. The reason for weight is primarily a gravitational attraction between the masses of the two bodies. The SI unit for weight is the Newton. In general, we will be concerned with situations in which bodies with mass are located where the free-fall acceleration is g. In these situations, we may say that the magnitude of the weight vector is: W = mg. As a vector, weight can be expressed as either = -mgj = -Wj, in which +j is the direction on the axis pointing away from the earth; or as = mg.

Techniques for weighing objects:
In almost every situation, we will assume that objects are being weighed from an inertial reference frame (that is, a case in which reference points are moving at a constant velocity).

If, however, weight is measured from a non-inertial frame, it will be referred to as apparent weight rather than actual weight. Objects are typically weighed by placing them on one pan of an equal-arm balance, and then adding reference weights to the other side until a balance is struck. Often, though, objects can be more conveniently weighed by being attached to a spring, and then hung, such that the force they exert on the spring causes a pointer to move along a scale. Of course, this form of measurement can only be accurate if g is the same as it was when the scale was calibrated.

Tension

Any time a cord is attached to a body and pulled so that it is taut, we may say that the cord is under tension. This force is pointed away from the body and along the cord at the point of attachment. It is generally expressed as T. In simple considerations of tension, the cord is generally assumed to be both without mass and incapable of stretching. In other words, its only role is as the connector between two other bodies. Even if both body and cord are accelerating, the cord is assumed to pull on both ends with the same magnitude of tension. This is also assumed to be the case in situations where the cord runs around a pulley; unless circumstances are clearly or purposefully otherwise, pulleys are assumed to have both negligible mass and negligible friction.

Newton's laws

First law:
Before Newton formulated his laws of mechanics, it was generally thought that some force had to act on an object continuously in order for it to move at a constant velocity. This seems to make sense: when an object is briefly pushed, it will eventually come to a rest. Newton, however, determined that unless some other force acted on the object (most notably friction or air resistance), it would continue in the direction it was pushed at the same velocity forever. In this light, a body at rest and a body in motion are not all that different, and, indeed, Newton's first law makes little distinction. It states that a body at

rest will tend to remain at rest, while a body in motion will tend to remain in motion. One fact that emerges from this law is that if the net force on an object is zero, it will be possible to find reference frames in which the body has no acceleration.

Second law:

Newton's second law is generally just written in equation form: $\sum F = ma$. Of course, in order to competently apply this equation, one needs to be certain what body it is being applied to. Once this is done, we may say that ΣF is the vector sum (that is, the net force) of all forces acting on that body. This measure only includes those forces that are external to the body; any internal forces, in which one part of the body exerts force on another, are discounted. Newton's second law somewhat encapsulates his first, because it entails that if no force acts on a body, then the body will not accelerate.

Third law:

Newton's third law of mechanics is quite simple: for every force, there is an equal and opposite force. When a hammer strikes a nail, the nail hits the hammer just as hard. If we consider two objects, A and B, then we may express any contact between these two bodies with the equation: $F_{AB} = -F_{BA}$. It is important to note in this kind of equation that the order of the subscripts denotes which body is exerting the force. Although the two forces are often referred to as the action and reaction forces, in physics there is really no such thing: there is no implication of cause and effect in the equation for Newton's third law. At first glance, this law might seem to forbid any movement at all; we must remember, however, that these equal, opposite forces are exerted on different bodies with different masses, and so they will not cancel each other out.

Static and kinetic frictional force

In order to illustrate the concept of friction, let us imagine a book resting on a table. As it sits there, the force of its weight (W) is equal and opposite to the normal force (N). If, however, we were to exert a force (F) on the book, attempting to push it to one side, a frictional force (f) would arise equal and opposite to our force. This kind of frictional force is known as static frictional force. As we increase our force on the book, however, we will eventually cause it to accelerate in the direction of our force. At this point, the frictional force opposing us will be known as kinetic frictional force. For the most part, kinetic frictional force is lower than static frictional force, and so the amount of force needed to maintain the movement of the book will be less than that needed to initiate movement.

Friction

The mysterious force known as friction is really just the force exerted by the surface atoms of one object on those of another. In situations where extremely flat and polished metal surfaces are brought into contact with one another in a vacuum, friction can be so great as to effectively weld the pieces of metal together. Most of the time, though, even surfaces that appear flat to the human eye are not really flat enough to create that much friction. Instead, only the very tops of two surfaces will touch one another. As an object is pulled across another, millions of tiny ruptures will occur on a microscopic level, as the peaks of one surface are ground against the peaks of the other.

Properties:
In describing the basic properties of friction during contact between two bodies, we are assuming that both bodies are dry and unlubricated, and that a force (F) is attempting to slide one body across the surface of the other.

The first property of friction is that, if the body does not move, then the static frictional force is exactly equal and opposite to F. Static frictional force has a maximum value, however, which is expressed as: $f_{s,max} = \mu_s N$, in which μ_s is the coefficient of static friction, and N is the magnitude of the normal force. If the magnitude of the component of F that is parallel to he surface should exceed the maximum value of static friction, the body will begin to move.

Once a body has begun to slide along the surface of another, the frictional force will decrease. In other words, an object's kinetic frictional force will always be less than the maximum value of the static frictional force. The value to which kinetic frictional force will diminish can be expressed as: $f_k = \mu_k N$, in which μ_k is known as the coefficient of kinetic friction. This coefficient (as well as the coefficient derived in the equation for maximum static friction) is without dimension. Since its value depends on the interaction of the body and the surface, it is usually described as existing "between" them.

Drag force

A drag force occurs when a body moves through some fluid (either liquid or gas) and experiences a force that opposes the motion of the body and is exerted in the direction in which the fluid is moving relative to the body. For the most part, basic physics sticks to cases in which a solid object is moving through air. In such cases, drag force (D) is related to the relative speed (v) by some experimentally determined drag coefficient, and can be found using the equation: $D = \frac{1}{2}C\rho A v^2$, in which ρ is the air density (mass per volume) and A is the effective cross-sectional area of the body (that is, the area of a cross-section of the body that runs perpendicular to v). Obviously, the higher the drag force, the lower the velocity.

Terminal speed

When a body falls through the air, its drag force will gradually increase until it equals the body's weight, at which point the downward acceleration of the body will be zero. The velocity of the body will thus not rise beyond a certain point, known as the terminal velocity. The equation for terminal velocity can be found by setting D = mg in the equation for drag force, and thus obtaining the equation: $\frac{1}{2}C\rho A v_t^2 = mg$. This equation can be rearranged as: $v_t = \sqrt{\frac{2mg}{C\rho A}}$.

Centripetal force

Objects moving in a circle, or in a circular arc around some center, are in fact accelerating towards that center at a rate equal to the velocity of the object squared divided by the radius of the circle. In order to account for the existence of this centripetal acceleration, we must posit a centripetal force acting on the body in the direction of the center of the circle. The magnitude of this force is constant for uniform motion, and it is derived from Newton's second law: $F = ma = \frac{mv^2}{r}$. Centripetal force (like centripetal acceleration) is a vector with a constant magnitude but a constantly changing direction.

Electromagnetic and gravitational forces

Physics tends to discuss forces individually (for instance, as weight, tension, drag, or normal), but in a more general scheme there are only two different kinds of force: gravitational and electromagnetic. Weight is the only common example of a gravitational force; all the rest are electromagnetic. Friction, drag, contact, and tension, are all at the most fundamental level electromagnetic forces exerted by one atom on another. When we examine the tension in a taut piece of rope, for instance, what we are really examining is the attractive force between the atoms of the rope. When we consider friction, we are

- 23 -

really considering the contact made by attracting atoms on the very surface of two objects moving relative to one another.

Small forces of nature

Besides the basic electromagnetic forces that can be observed, there are some that occur on such a small scale that they are impossible to detect without sophisticated equipment. For instance, physicists have demonstrated the presence of the so-called weak force, which is involved in some forms of radioactive decay; and the strong force, which holds together the contents of an atomic nucleus. Scientists have spent a great deal of time working to reduce the number of small forces to some single force, and indeed it has been shown that electromagnetic force and weak force are both part of a comprehensive electroweak force. There is still a great deal of labor being expended to unify the various forces into one over-arching superforce.

Work

Basic equation:

The equation for work (W) is fairly simple: W = Fd, where F is the magnitude of the force exerted and d is the displacement of the object on which the force is exerted. For this simple equation, the force vector and the displacement vector have the same direction. If this is not the case, however, then the equation can be rewritten: $W = Fd \cos \phi$. In turn, this equation can be rearranged to $W = (d)(F \cos \phi) = (F)(d \cos \phi)$, so that it is clear that work can be calculated in a couple of different ways. If force and direction have the same direction, then work is positive; if they are in opposite directions, however, work is negative; and, if they are perpendicular, work done by the force is zero.

Scalar:

Even though the two factors used to derive work (force and displacement) are vectors, work itself is a scalar. Typically, work is expressed in the SI units Newton-meters, or joules. In the British system of measurement, the unit of work is the foot-pound. Oftentimes, though, when dealing with atoms or subatomic particles, physicists will use the electron-volt (eV) as the unit of work. The relation of the electron-volt to the joule is: 1 electron-volt $= 1.60 X 10^{-19} J$. If more than one force is doing work on an object, then each of these forces must be calculated individually, and the total derived from the sum.

One-dimensional analysis:

If we consider the work performed by a variable force in one dimension, then we are assuming that the direction of the force and of the displacement are the same. The magnitude of the force will depend on the position of the particle. In order to calculate the amount of work performed by a variable force over a given distance, we should first divide the total displacement into a number of intervals, each with a width of Δx. We may then say that the amount of work performed during any one interval is: $\Delta W = \overline{F(x)} \Delta x$. We can then say that the total amount of wok performed is the sum of all work performed in the various intervals: $W = \int_{x_i}^{x_f} F(x) dx$. Obviously, the smaller we can make the intervals, the more exact our measure of work will be.

Three-dimensional analysis:

If an object is acted on by a three dimensional force, then this force will have to be calculated along all three axes: $F = F_x i + F_y j + F_z k$. We can assume that the amount of force will vary according to the position of the particle, and that the object will move through some incremental displacement: $dr = dxi + dyj + dzk$. If this is the case, then the increment of work done on the object during some displacement (dr) is: $dW = F \cdot dr = F_x dx + F_y dy + F_z dz$. So, with this in place, we can say that the total amount of work performed through the full displacement is: $W = \int_{r_i}^{r_f} dW = \int_{x_i}^{x_f} F_x dx + \int_{y_i}^{y_f} F_y dy + \int_{z_i}^{z_f} F_z dz$. We can note that if F has only one component, this equation can be reduced to the one for work by a variable force in one dimension.

Work performed by a spring:

The work performed by a spring is one of the classic examples of work performed by variable force. When a spring is neither compressed nor extended, we may say that it is in a relaxed state. Any time the spring is taken out of this state, whether by being stretched or compressed, it will exert what is called a restoring force, as it attempts to reclaim its relaxed state. In most cases, we can say that the force (F) exerted by the spring is proportional to the displacement of the free end from its position during the relaxed state. This is known as Hooke's law, and is expressed: $F = -kd$. The negative sign in this equation indicates that the force is always opposite to the displacement. The constant k is known as the spring constant, and is a measure of the resilience of the spring.

If we extend an axis running parallel to the length of a spring, we may make this adjustment to Hooke's law: $F = -kx$. If we are then to move a block attached to a spring from point x_i to point x_j, we may be said to be doing work on the block as the spring is also doing work on the block. To determine the work done by the spring on the block, we can substitute F from Hooke's law into our equation for determining work performed by a variable force, and arrive at this measure: $W = \frac{1}{2}kx_i^2 - \frac{1}{2}kx_f^2$. This work will be positive if $x_i^2 > x_j^2$, and negative if the opposite. If $x_i = 0$ and we decide to call the final position x, then we may change our equation: $W = -\frac{1}{2}kx^2$.

Kinetic energy

When we see an object in motion, we assume that work has been performed on it. The kinetic energy of the object is that quality of its motion that can be related in a qualitative way to the amount of work performed on the object. Kinetic energy can be defined:

$K = \dfrac{1}{2}mv^2$, in which m is mass and v is speed. Kinetic energy cannot be negative, since it depends on the square of speed (and since mass can never be negative). Units for kinetic energy are the same as for work: joules. Kinetic energy is a scalar quantity; it does not have direction.

Work-kinetic energy theorem:
Changes in kinetic will occur when a force (F) does work (W) on an object, such that the speed of the object is altered. This change in kinetic energy is equal to the amount of work that is done, and can be expressed: $W = K_f - K_i = \Delta K$ or $K_f = K_i + W$. This equation is commonly referred to as the work-kinetic energy theorem. If there are several different forces acting on the object, then W in this equation is simply the total work done by all the forces, or the net force. This equation can be very helpful in solving some problems that otherwise would rely solely on Newton's laws of motion.

An object in free fall:
One interesting application of the work-kinetic energy theorem is on objects in a free fall. To begin with, let us assert that the force acting on such an object is its weight, equal to its mass times g. The work done by this force will be positive, as the force is exerted in the direction in which the object is traveling. Kinetic energy will therefore increase, according to the work-kinetic energy theorem. If the object is dropped from such a great height that it eventually reaches its terminal velocity, then the drag force will be equal to the weight, and so the total amount of work exerted on the object will be zero. According to the work-kinetic energy theorem, this means that the kinetic energy of the object will remain constant.

Proof of the work-kinetic energy theorem:
The work-kinetic energy theorem is a direct consequence of Newton's second law of motion. Though it applies to objects moving in three dimensions, we shall confine ourselves to proving its motion through one. We also assume that the magnitude of force

may vary. If we take an object of mass m moving along the x-axis, and acted on b a force F(x) in the positive direction of that axis, we may say that the work performed during the displacement from point i to point j is: $W = \int_{x_i}^{x_f} F(x)dx = \int_{x_i}^{x_f} madx$. Here, Newton's second law is used so that we may substitute ma for F(x). We may then adjust the value for ma dx in the equation as: $madx = m\dfrac{dv}{dt}dx$.

We were left with the equation $madx = m\dfrac{dv}{dt}dx$, in which Newton's second law had been used to modify the equation used for work performed by a variable force. Moving ahead, we may use the so-called "chain rule" of calculus, and construct: $\dfrac{dv}{dt} = \dfrac{dv}{dx}\dfrac{dx}{dt} = \dfrac{dv}{dx}v$. Having done this, the equation becomes $madx = m\dfrac{dv}{dx}vdx = mvdv$. If we then take this equation and substitute it into our original equation, we arrive at $W = \int_{v_i}^{v_f} mvdv = m\int_{v_i}^{v_f} vdv = \dfrac{1}{2}mv_f^2 - \dfrac{1}{2}mv_i^2$. We should note that m can be moved outside of the integral, since it is a constant. If we can recognize the terms on the right side of this equation as kinetic energies, we may arrive at the work-kinetic energy theorem: $W = K_f - K_i = \Delta K$.

Power

Power, put simply, is the rate at which work is done. Power, like work, is a scalar quantity. If know that the amount of work W has been performed in a given amount of time Δt, then we may find average power: $\overline{P} = \dfrac{W}{\Delta t}$. If, on the other hand, we are looking for the instantaneous power, we can find it: $P = \dfrac{dW}{dt}$. Power is typically expressed in joules per seconds, more commonly as watts. Sometimes, it may be better to express the rate at which work is done in terms of the force and the velocity of the body. If this is the case, power may found as $P = Fv$, in which P is the instantaneous power and v is the speed of the object.

Reference frames

In order to correctly apply Newton's mechanical laws, we must be sure that motion is taking place within inertial reference frames (those which are moving at a constant speed with respect to one another). Some of the quantities in physics will be the same even of they are measured by observers in different reference frames. These are called invariant quantities, and include force, mass, acceleration, and time. If an observer measures an object's mass, for instance, every other observer in every other reference frame will get the same measure for the object's mass. Other physical quantities, like velocity and displacement, will be measured differently by different observers, and so are called variant quantities.

Principle of invariance:

Over time, physicists have adopted what is now known as the principle of invariance: that is, the idea that the laws of physics will have the same form in all inertial reference frames. This applies even though some physical quantities (like velocity and displacement) may differ between reference frames. For instance, the work-kinetic energy theorem should hold true even though different observers in different reference frames might derive different measurements for work and kinetic energy. The idea behind the principle of invariance is simply that each of these observers will find that the laws of physics work in the recognizable way in his or her reference frame.

Energy

Energy is a word that has found a million different uses in the English language, but in physics it really just refers to a measure made on one or more bodies. By assessing either its behavior or its configuration, we may be able to measure the amount of energy in a body or group of bodies. There are various kinds of energy: kinetic energy is associated with motion; potential energy is the energy associated with particular arrangements of bodies;

thermal energy is associated with the random movements of the atoms and molecules in a body; mechanical energy is the sum of an object's kinetic and potential energy.

Potential energy:

Potential energy is the amount of energy that can be ascribed to a body or bodies based on configuration. There are a couple of different kinds of potential energy.

- Gravitational potential energy is the energy associated with the separation of bodies that are attracted to one another gravitationally. Any time you lift an object above the ground, you are increasing the gravitational potential energy of that object.

- Another kind of potential energy is elastic potential energy; elastic potential energy is associated with the compression or expansion of an elastic, or spring-like, object. Physicists will often refer to potential energy as being "stored" within a body, the implication being that it could emerge in the future.

Mechanical energy:

Mechanical energy is the sum of kinetic and potential energy. If a spring is compressed by an object of mass m hitting it with kinetic energy K, then we can set up Hooke's law to assess the result: $F(x) = -kx$, where x is the amount that the spring is compressed. The block will compress the spring, and then the spring will restore itself to its original state. So, while the spring is being compressed, it gains potential energy as the block loses kinetic energy. The change in energy is equal and opposite, and can be expressed: $\Delta K + \Delta U = 0$, where U is the potential energy. The mechanical energy of the entire block-spring system is constant throughout.

Gravitational force:

If we imagine a ball with mass m moving perpendicular to the surface of the earth, with its weight the only force acting on it (mg). As the ball rises, the weight will be doing work on the ball, decreasing its speed and its kinetic energy, and slowing it down until it momentarily stops. During this ascent, the potential energy of the ball will be rising. Once the ball begins to fall back down, it will lose potential energy as it gains kinetic. We can say then that as the ball rises energy is transferred from the ball to the ball-earth system, and as the ball falls energy is transferred from the ball-earth system back to the ball. In this relation, mechanical energy is conserved throughout; the potential energy of the ball at its height is equal to the kinetic energy of the ball at its lowest point.

Kinetic frictional energy:

In systems where friction or air resistance is negligible, it is easy to construct systems in which mechanical energy is conserved. However, if we take friction into account, we arrive at a different sort of result. For example, let us imagine a block with mass m sliding across the floor until it comes to a stop due to friction. Unlike a compressed spring or a ball flung into the air, there is no way for this ball to regain its energy with a return trip. Therefore, we cannot say that the lost kinetic energy is being stored as potential energy. Instead, it is dissipated, meaning that its transfer cannot be reversed. In general, we must admit that the mechanical energy of the block-floor system has been not conserved but reduced.

Determining potential energy

Arriving at a quantitative measure for potential energy is not unlike the operation for kinetic energy. If a force F works on an object and accomplishes work W, then we may modify the work-kinetic energy theorem to read: $\Delta U = -W$. In other words, whenever a force changes the potential energy of a system by changing its configuration, the change in potential energy is the negative of the work accomplished by that force. For one-dimensional energy, we may say: $\Delta U = -W = -\int_{x_i}^{x} F(x)dx$. To find the potential energy of some configuration x, we can use this equation: $U(x) = U(x_0) + \Delta U = U(x_0) - \int_{x_0}^{x} F(X)dx$.

Elastic potential energy equations:

In order to produce the amount of elastic potential energy in a compressed or stretched spring, we should declare x_0 the reference configuration; that is, the spring in its relaxed state. Potential energy in this state is zero. If we substitute Hooke's law into our equation for determining potential energy, we arrive at: $U(x) = \dfrac{1}{2}kx^2$, where x is any elongation or compression of the spring. If we imagine a block pushed against the spring and then shifted back to its original position, we can describe the block spring system: $\dfrac{1}{2}kx^2 + \dfrac{1}{2}mv^2 = E$. Throughout all of these equations, total mechanical energy is the same.

Gravitational potential energy equations:

If we imagine an object moving perpendicular to the surface of the earth (and therefore only acted upon by the gravitational force), then the force acting on it can be expressed: $F(y) = -mg$, with the negative sign indicating that the force tends downward. Assuming, then, that y_0 is the point at which potential energy is zero, we can say: $U(y) = mgy$. Expanded to represent the entire particle-earth system, this equation is: $mgy + \dfrac{1}{2}mv^2 = E$. In both of these equations, the total mechanical energy of the ball-earth system will remain constant.

Force of the potential energy curve

If we suppose that an object is constrained so that it moves only along a single, x-axis, then we can develop a plot of its potential energy U(x) as a function of its position on this axis. In order to do this, however, we need to be able to find the force once we have been given the potential energy function. This is done by starting with the equation that defines potential energy: $\Delta U = -W$. If we assume one-dimensional motion, the work done by the force moving the particle through Δx is $F(x)\Delta x$. If we plug this into the equation for potential energy and rearrange for F(x), we arrive at: $F(x) = -\dfrac{dU(x)}{dx}$.

Conservative and nonconservative forces

Forces that change the state of a system by changing the amount of potential energy are called conservative forces. Every other kind of force is considered non-conservative. One

- 32 -

test of whether a force is conservative is found by considering the path of a ball thrown straight up into the air. Since the ball has the exact same amount of kinetic energy when it returns to its original location (known as completing its closed path), it can be said to be conservative. More generally, a force can be said to be conservative if the work it does on an object through a closed path is zero. Frictional force would not meet this standard, of course, because it does not encourage an object to complete a closed path.

Another way to consider whether a force is conservative or nonconservative is to imagine an object moving from point to point b along path 1, and the moving back to a along path 2. If the force that moves this object is conservative, then the work done on this round-trip must be zero: $W_{ab,1} + W_{ba,2} = 0$, or $W_{ab,1} = -W_{ba,2}$. If we allow motion to go along path 2 exclusively, we may say: $W_{ab,2} = -W_{ba,2}$. From these two equations, we may arrive at: $W_{ab,1} = W_{ab,2}$. Therefore, we may say that a force is conservative if the work it does on an object to move it between two points is the same no matter the path taken between those two points.

Conservation of energy

If we consider a block and spring system (in which a block with mass m slides against a spring which is compressed, and then returns to its natural resting state), we will see that the oscillations of the spring decrease until they become zero, as the spring returns to its resting state. This decrease in kinetic energy will happen as the thermal energy of the block and the ground beneath it increase. This change in thermal energy is expressed: ΔE_{int}, because thermal energy is an internal force. If we then expand our system so that it includes block, spring, and floor, we may express the conservation of energy as: $\Delta K + \Delta U + \Delta E_{int} = 0$. This is only appropriate for an isolated system, however: in a strict sense, most systems will involve numerous additional energy quantities.

We have seen that energy, though it may change form, will be neither created nor destroyed during physical processes. If we construct a system, however, and some external force performs work on it, we can measure this work as: $W = \Delta K + \Delta U + \Delta E_{int}$. If the work is positive, then the overall store of energy is increased; if it is negative, however, we can say that the overall energy of the system has decreased. Most of the time, physicists who notice that an external force is regularly influencing a system will simply enlarge the system to include the external force. Though there have been many cases in which physicists did not know what force was influencing an external object, there have never been any cases in which the law of conservation of energy has been found to be violated.

Work done by frictional forces

Let us imagine a block with mass m that is sliding along a horizontal floor, acted on by a constant nonconservative force f and a constant conservative force F. Both of these forces are acting against the motion of the block. We will take the block as our system, even though this system is regularly affected by the two external forces. We can then apply Newton's second law to the block, and say that, along its line of motion: $\sum F = -F - f = ma$. Since the forces are constant, the deceleration of the block is also constant, and can be figured: $v_f^2 = v_i^2 + 2ad$, or $a = \dfrac{v_f^2 - v_i^2}{2d}$. We can rearrange this to find the kinetic energy of the block: $-Fd - fd = \dfrac{1}{2}mv_f^2 - \dfrac{1}{2}mv_i^2 = \Delta K$.

If we rearrange our equation for the kinetic energy of our sliding block such that we are now solving for the nonconservative frictional force, will look like this: $-fd = \Delta K + \Delta U = \Delta E$. In other words, the amount of kinetic frictional force is equal to the amount of mechanical energy lost by the block system. This makes sense, given the law of conservation of energy. The product –fd is a negative because frictional force is exerted in the direction opposite to displacement; for this reason, as we would expect, ΔE is negative. It should be noted that the left side of the above equation is not the same as the work one on the block by the frictional force. This is because the sum of all of the complicated frictional forces is not the same as f, the average of these forces.

Center of mass

It is one thing to chart the motion of a spherical object: when a ball is tossed into the air, anyone can observe the parabolic path that it makes. When a stick is thrown into the air, however, the movement appears much more complex. Nevertheless, the stick will have what is known as a center of mass, a point which will move in the same parabolic path. For an object like a stick, the center of mass is located at the place where the stick can be balanced on your finger. Every single body has a center of mass. One interesting way to demonstrate this would be to place a light at the center of mass of a stick, then turn off the lights and throw the stick into the air; the light would seem to make a very regular path in the air.

Simple systems of particles (two-dimensions):
In beginning to consider some of the physical problems associated with center of mass, we might take the example of two particles. These two particles, with masses m_1 and m_2, will have a center of mass that can be located with this equation: $x_{cm} = \dfrac{m_2}{m_{1+}m_2}d$, where d is the distance between the two particles. If the particles are shifted on the coordinate plane, such that neither of them is at the origin, we can find the center of mass: $x_{cm} = \dfrac{m_1x_1 + m_2x_2}{m_1 + m_2}$.

This equation can be rewritten: $x_{cm} = \dfrac{m_1x_1 + m_2x_2}{M}$.

Simple systems of particles (three dimensions):
If we are attempting to determine the center of mass for a group of particles spread out over three dimensions, then we must have a reading for each of the three coordinates:

$x_{cm} = \frac{1}{M} \sum_{i=1}^{n} m_i x_i$, $y_{cm} = \frac{1}{M} \sum_{i=1}^{n} m_i y_i$, and $z_{cm} = \frac{1}{M} \sum_{i=1}^{n} m_i z_i$. This center of mass could also be defined

through the use of vectors; first the position of each particle is indexed: $r_i = x_i i + y_i j + z_i k$;

then, the position of the center of mass can be given as: $r_{cm} = x_{cm} i + y_{cm} i + z_{cm} k$; finally, the three

scalar equations we used before can be replaced by this vector equation: $r_{cm} = \frac{1}{M} \sum_{i=1}^{n} m_i r_i$.

Rigid bodies:

Many objects, for instance a stick, have so many atoms that that they can be effectively

treated as a single, continuous distribution of matter. In order to find the center of mass of

such a body, then, we must make the particles into differential mass elements (dm), and the

coordinates of the center of mass into: $x_{cm} = \frac{1}{M} \int x\, dm$, $y_{cm} = \frac{1}{M} \int y\, dm$, and $z_{cm} = \frac{1}{M} \int z\, dm$.

Although we technically should evaluate the integrals for all the mass elements in the

object, we will instead just rewrite them in terms of the coordinates of the mass elements.

So, if an object has uniform density, we can write: $\frac{dm}{dV} = \frac{M}{V}$. Then, substituting dm from the

first equation, we find: $x_{cm} = \frac{1}{V} \int x\, dV$, $y_{cm} = \frac{1}{V} \int y\, dV$, and $z_{cm} = \frac{1}{V} \int z\, dV$.

Newton's second law and systems of particles

If we were to consider two billiard balls as a system, and then to strike one billiard ball off

of the other in a straight line, we could say that the center of mass of this system continues

its forward progress uninterrupted by the collision between the two balls. This can be

more closely at a molecular level: if we take a group of n particles and study their collective

motion, we will find that the center of mass moves in a way that is identical to a unified

body with an equal mass: this center of mass can be given a position, velocity, and

acceleration. The vector equation that describes the motion of such systems of particles is:

$\sum F_{ext} = M a_{cm}$. This, of course, is Newton's second law.

The behavior of the center of mass of a system of particles can be described with a modified form of Newton's second law: $\sum F_{ext} = Ma_{cm}$. In this equation, ΣF_{ext} is the vector sum of all the external forces that act on the system; M is the total mass of the system, and a_{cm} is the acceleration of the center of mass. Like all vector equations, this is equivalent to three scalar equations, one for each component: $\sum F_{ext,x} = Ma_{cm,x}$, $\sum F_{ext,y} = Ma_{cm,y}$, and $\sum F_{ext,z} = Ma_{cm,z}$. This equation will apply not only to systems of particles, but also to solid bodies.

Proof of Newton's second law:

To prove Newton's second law as it governs systems of particles, we may begin by stating that for such a system: $Mr_{cm} = m_1 r_1 + m_2 r_2 + ... + m_n r_n$, in which M is the total mass of the system and r_{cm} is the vector that describes the position of the center of mass. If we differentiate with respect to time, we get: $Mv_{cm} = m_1 v_1 + m_2 v_2 + ... + m_n v_n$. If we then differentiate this with respect to time, we get: $Ma_{cm} = m_1 a_1 + m_2 a_2 + ... + m_n a_n$. We then have a position, velocity, and acceleration for the center of mass, and we can substitute using Newton's second law (F = ma) to arrive at: $Ma_{cm} = F_1 + F_2 + ... + F_n$. The right side of this equation will contain both internal and external forces; the internal forces will cancel each other out, and all that will remain is the vector sum of external forces: $\sum F_{ext} = Ma_{cm}$.

Linear momentum

In physics, linear momentum can be found by multiplying the mass and velocity of a particle: $p = mv$. Momentum and velocity will always be in the same direction. Newton's second law describes momentum, stating that the rate of change of momentum is proportional to the force exerted, and is in the direction of the force. In equation form, then: $\sum F = \dfrac{dp}{dt}$. If we substitute p into the original equation, we get:

$$\sum F = \frac{dp}{dt} = \frac{d}{dt}(mv) = m\frac{dv}{dt} = ma$$, giving us a couple of different approaches for finding linear momentum in classical mechanics.

System of particles:

If we are to take a system of particles with a total linear momentum of P, then we may find

this total linear momentum: $P = Mv_{cm}$, in which the total mass of the system is multiplied by

the velocity of the system's center of mass. Taking the time derivative of this equation

gives us: $\dfrac{dP}{dt} = M\dfrac{dv_{cm}}{dt} = Ma_{cm}$. If we look at this equation alongside the equation for the force

associated with a system of particles, $\sum F_{ext} = Ma_{cm}$, we will find that Newton's second law

can be applied with respect to particles with the following: $\sum F_{ext} = \dfrac{dP}{dt}$, which is essentially

just a generalization of the equation for a single particle.

Conservation:

If we assume a closed and isolated system (that is, one in which no particles leave or enter,

and upon which the sum of external forces is zero), then we can assume that the

momentum of the system will neither increase nor decrease. That is, if we write the

equation for the linear momentum of the system such that $\sum F_{ext} = 0$, then we will find that

P is a constant. The law of conservation of linear momentum applies universally in physics,

even in situations of extremely high velocity or subatomic particles. The equation for linear

momentum is a vector equation, and as such it could be divided into three component

equations.

Collision

Most people have a general idea of what the word collision means. In physics, however, the

word has a more specialized meaning: it is an isolated event in which a relatively strong

force acts on each of two or more colliding bodies for a relatively short period of time. In

order for a collision to be subject to study, it must have a clear beginning, occurrence, and

end. Technically, a collision does not have to entail contact between the two bodies; a

satellite that is violently influenced by the proximity of an astronomical body may be said

to collide with it without actually touching it. One of the most basic ways in which physicists conduct research is by causing a collision between two bodies, and investigating the changes that this collision produces.

Elastic collisions:

During a collision, the center of mass of the system continues moving, unaffected by the violence of the collision. This is because the linear momentum of the system is unchanged by the collision: $P = Mv_{cm} = (m_1 + m_2)v_{cm}$. The velocity of the center of mass can be found:

$v_{cm} = \dfrac{P}{m_1 + m_2} = \dfrac{m_1}{m_1 + m_2}v_{1i}$. If both bodies are moving before an elastic collision, then the conservation of linear momentum equation can be rewritten: $m_1v_{1i} + m_2v_{2i} = m_1v_{1f} + m_2v_{2f}$; and

the conservation of kinetic energy equation: $\dfrac{1}{2}m_1v_{1i}^2 + \dfrac{1}{2}m_2v_{2i}^2 = \dfrac{1}{2}m_1v_{1f}^2 + \dfrac{1}{2}m_2v_{2f}^2$. These equations

can be adjusted to yield the initial and final velocities: $v_{1f} = \dfrac{m_1 - m_2}{m_1 + m_2}v_{1i} + \dfrac{2m_2}{m_1 + m_2}v_{2i}$ and

$v_{2f} = \dfrac{2m_1}{m_1 + m_2}v_{1i} + \dfrac{m_2 - m_1}{m_1 + m_2}v_{2i}$.

Inelastic collisions:

If the kinetic energy of a system of colliding bodies is conserved, the collision is considered inelastic. If the kinetic energy is completely transferred to other forms of energy, as for instance when a ball of putty hits the floor, it is called a completely inelastic collision. Considering, then, a system in which one body is initially stationary, we may say that the law of conservation of linear momentum will hold true: $m_1v = (m_1 + m_2)V$. If both bodies are moving at the time of collision, we may say: $m_1v_1 + m_2v_2 = (m_1 + m_2)V$. In inelastic collisions, the kinetic energy is usually converted into thermal energy.

Collisions in two dimensions:

When colliding bodies glance off of one another, meaning that they move at an angle after collision, they are said to be colliding in two dimensions. In studying such collisions, physicists will refer to an impact parameter, the distance by which a collision fails to be head-on. Such collisions will have both an x and a y component, and their equations for linear momentum can be written: $m_1 v_{1i} = m_1 v_{1f} \cos\theta_1 + m_2 v_{2f} \cos\theta_2$ (x-component), and

$0 = -m_1 v_{1f} \sin\theta_1 + m_2 v_{2f} \sin\theta_2$ (y-component), in which θ_1 and θ_2 are the angles at which the two bodies depart after collision. If we are studying an elastic collision in two dimensions, we can say that kinetic energy is conserved: $\frac{1}{2} m_1 v_{1i}^2 = \frac{1}{2} m_1 v_{1f}^2 + \frac{1}{2} m_2 v_{2f}^2$.

Types of motion

When a body is moving in a straight line, it is said in physics to be moving in translation. When, on the other hand, it is moving around some fixed axis, it is said to be in rotation. It is important to note this word "fixed"; a rolling ball cannot be said to be in rotation, because its axis is moving. For a rotating object, the fixed axis is called the axis of rotation, or rotation axis. Every point of the body will move in a circle that has this axis as its center, and every point will move through the same angle over the same interval of time. By contrast, during translation every point of the body will move at the same speed, and will cover the same amount of linear distance over the same interval of time.

Angular position in rotation:
In order to describe the motion of a rotating body, physicists will often draw a reference line that is perpendicular to the rotation axis and is rotating with the body. The motion of the body can then be described by determining the angular position of this line, which can be found: $\theta = \frac{s}{r}$, where s is the length of the arc of any circle cut by the x-axis and the reference line, and r is the radius of that circle. This angle is measured in radians; there are 2π radians in each circle. The angle does not get reset to zero with each complete rotation. In cases of pure rotation, we can know everything about the body if we only know $\theta(t)$, its angular position of the body's reference line as a function of time.

Angular displacement in rotation:

If we consider a rotating body in which the reference line changes its position from θ_1 to θ_2, we may say that the body has undergone an angular displacement that can be calculated: $\Delta\theta = \theta_2 - \theta_1$. This definition of angular displacement will apply not only to the body itself, but to every particle within that body. If a body was in translational motion, then we could say that its displacement is either positive or negative, depending on which direction the body is moving. In a similar way, physicists describe the displacement of a rotating body as positive if the body is rotating counterclockwise, and negative if the body is rotating clockwise.

Angular velocity in rotation:

If we are able to determine the angular position of the reference line of a rotating body at the beginning and end of a given interval of time, we may calculate the average angular velocity of the body as: $\overline{\omega} = \dfrac{\theta_2 - \theta_1}{t_2 - t_1} = \dfrac{\Delta\theta}{\Delta t}$. Instantaneous angular velocity, on the other hand, is the limit of the ratio in the above equation as the time interval is brought as close as possible to zero: $\omega = \lim\limits_{\Delta t \to 0} \dfrac{\Delta\theta}{\Delta t} = \dfrac{d\theta}{dt}$. As long as we know the angular position of the body as a function of time (that is, $\theta(t)$), we can find the angular velocity by differentiation. This description of angular velocity holds not only for the body as a whole but for every particle within that body. As with angular displacement, angular velocity can be either positive or negative depending on whether the body is rotating clockwise (negative) or counterclockwise (positive).

Angular acceleration in rotation:

If the angular velocity of a body is not constant, then that body can be said to have an angular acceleration. So, if we can find the two different velocities at the beginning and end of an interval of time, we can calculate average angular acceleration: $\overline{\alpha} = \dfrac{\omega_2 - \omega_1}{t_2 - t_1} = \dfrac{\Delta\omega}{\Delta t}$. Instantaneous angular acceleration, on the other hand, is the limit of this average quantity as we decrease the time interval as close as possible to zero: $\alpha = \lim\limits_{\Delta t \to 0} \dfrac{\Delta \omega}{\Delta t} = \dfrac{dw}{dt}$. The measure of angular acceleration holds not only for the body as a whole but for every particle within that body. Typically, angular acceleration is given in radians per second squared, or revolutions per second squared.

Rotation with constant angular acceleration:

Motion with a constant rate of acceleration is an important case in mechanics, so much so that there are special equations to describe it. This is true of bodies moving in translation as well as those moving in rotation. In the latter case, that is when angular acceleration is constant, we may simply modify the equations that describe linear motion with constant acceleration. Without the angle of displacement, we may use: $\omega = \omega_0 + \alpha t$. Without angular velocity: $\theta = \omega_0 t + \dfrac{1}{2}\alpha t^2$. Without time: $\omega^2 = \omega_0^2 + 2\alpha\theta$. Without acceleration: $\theta = \dfrac{1}{2}(\omega_0 + \omega)t$.

Linear and angular variables

When a rigid body is moving around an axis of rotation, every particle of that body will take the exact same amount of time to complete a full revolution; in other words, they will all have the same angular speed. Nevertheless, the farther away from the axis a particle is, the greater will be the circumference of its circle, and therefore its linear speed will be greater than that of a particle closer to the axis. Many times, physicists will need to compare the linear displacement, velocity, or acceleration of a particle with its angular displacement, velocity, or acceleration. In order to do this, they will need to know the perpendicular distance from the particle to the axis, which is the same thing as the radius of the circle traversed by the particle during rotation.

Position and speed:

If we are examining a body in rotation and see that a reference line has rotated through an angle θ, the displacement of a point on that line can be given as: $s = \theta r$, in which r is the radius drawn from the particle to the rotation axis. If we are to them differentiate this

equation with respect to time, we arrive at: $\dfrac{ds}{dt} = \dfrac{d\theta}{dt}r$. This equation amounts to saying that

the linear speed is equal to the angular speed multiplied by the radius: $v = \omega r$. We can see

that since all points in the body will have the same angular speed, their linear speed will

increase as their radius increases.

Acceleration:

If we take the equation $v = \omega r$ and differentiate according to time, we arrive at $\dfrac{dv}{dt} = \dfrac{d\omega}{dt}r$.

However, we should note that that the left side of this equation is only that part of the

linear acceleration that is responsible for changes in the magnitude of v. Like v, this part of

the linear acceleration is tangential to the path of the point, and is therefore known as the

tangential component a_t of the linear acceleration of the point, and we can write: $a_t = \alpha r$.

Linear acceleration will also have a radial component, which will be responsible for its

changes in direction: $a_r = \dfrac{v^2}{r} = \omega^2 r$.

Kinetic energy of rotation

When we determine the kinetic energy of a rigid body in rotation, we treat the body as a

collection of particles with different speeds, and we tally up kinetic energy: $K = \sum \dfrac{1}{2} m_i v_i^2$, in

which i is the number of different particles. Of course, the measure for velocity will not be

the same for all particles, so we substitute using our equation for linear and angular

velocity, and get: $K = \sum \dfrac{1}{2} m_i (\omega r_i)^2 = \dfrac{1}{2} \left(\sum m_i r_i^2 \right) \omega^2$. The quantity in parentheses on the right

side of the equation is known as the rotational inertia, and it describes how the mass is

distributed around the axis of rotation. We can then find kinetic energy as a radian

measure: $I = \sum m_i r_i^2$.

Calculating rotational inertia

If we are dealing with a rotating body made up of many discrete particles, we can calculate rotational inertia using this equation: $I = \sum m_i r_i^2$. If, however, the body is continuous, the sum of this equation can be replaced with an integral, and rotational inertia can be calculated: $I = \int r^2 dm$. For the most part, the rotational inertia of a body with respect to an axis will depend on three factors: the shape of the body; the perpendicular distance from the axis to the body's center of mass; and the orientation of the body with respect to the mass.

Parallel-axis theorem

If we happen to know the rotational inertia of a body around any axis passing through its center of mass, we can use the parallel-axis theorem to find the rotational inertia around any other axis parallel to this axis. This is done using the equation: $I = I_{cm} + Mh^2$, in which h is the perpendicular distance between the two axes. Another way to express this theorem is to say that the rotational inertia of a body around any axis will be equal to the rotational inertia it would have around that axis if all of its mass were concentrated at its center of mass, plus its rotational inertia about a parallel rotation axis through its center of mass.

Torque

Torque is the force that produces rotation in a body. In order to calculate the torque applied to a given body, we must know the radius (the distance from the point where the force is applied to the axis on which it rotates), the amount of force applied, and the angle to the radius at which it is applied. Specifically, we can calculate torque: $\tau = (r)(F \sin \phi)$. The SI unit for torque is the Newton-meter. A torque is positive if it tends to rotate the body counterclockwise, in the direction of increasing θ, and negative if it tends to rotate the body clockwise. In some cases the radius line will be extended through F; in these cases,

- 44 -

the extended line is known as the line of action of F, and the torque applied perpendicular to the extended line is called the moment arm of F.

Applied to particles:

The definition of torque can be modified such that it will apply to particles moving relative to a fixed point, and not just rigid bodies moving around a fixed axis. The particle need not move in a circle around the point for torque to apply. If, for instance, we consider particle P, which has its distance from the origin O described by the position vector r. A force F acts on P, causing vector r to lie at angle ϕ to vector F. The torque involved in this scenario can be calculated: $\tau = r \times F$, in which τ is perpendicular to the plane containing r and F.

Newton's second law and rotation

Let us consider a simple case of a rigid body rotating around a fixed axis. This rigid body consists of a mass m attached to a mass-less rod of length r. A force F acts on the particle, causing it to rotate. The torque can then be calculated: $\tau = m(\alpha r)r = (mr^2)\alpha$, with the bit in parentheses on the right being the rotational inertia. This equation reduces to $\tau = I\alpha$. If we create a situation in which more than one force is being applied to the particle, then we can extend this equation: $\sum \tau = I\alpha$, in which $\sum \tau$ is the net torque acting on the particle. This is the rotational version of Newton's second law.

Rotation equations

If we imagine a body with mass m and a mass-less rod attached to the axis. If the mass travels through a section of a revolution, then, we can say that the work done during this period is: $W = \int_{\theta_i}^{\theta_f} \tau d\theta$. The power of a rotational motion can be found with the equation: $P = \dfrac{dW}{dt} = \tau \dfrac{d\theta}{dt} = \tau \omega$. If we then want to use the work-kinetic energy theorem, we will find:

$W = \frac{1}{2}I\omega_f^2 - \frac{1}{2}I\omega_i^2 = K_f - K_i = \Delta K$. In words, we may say that the work done by the net torque acting on a rotating rigid body is equal to the change in the rotational kinetic energy of that body.

Rolling

When a body, like a bicycle wheel or a ball, is rolling, this means that it is experiencing both translation and rotation. Its center of mass will be moving forward at a constant speed v_{cm}. During time interval t the center of mass will move through distance s at the same time that a point on the edge of the body will traverse angle θ, such that $s = R\theta$, where r is the radius of the wheel. If we differentiate this equation with respect to time, we get: $v_{cm} = \omega R$. The motion of a rolling body may either be considered separately as translational or rotational, or these motions may be considered together.

One alternate way to look at rolling is as a pure rotation around an axis at the point where the rolling object contacts the ground. For instance, if we were to consider a bicycle wheel in this way, we would say that the rotation axis is at the point where the tire touches the street, and perpendicular to the plane of the wheel. Interestingly, if an observer were to calculate the angular speed of the wheel around this new axis, it would be found to be exactly the same as the angular speed of the wheel around the axis at its center of mass. For instance, if we were to call the wheel's radius R, we would say that the top is now a distance of 2R from the axis, and linear speed is $v_{top} = (\omega)(2R) = 2(\omega R) = 2v_{cm}$.

Kinetic energy:
In order to calculate the kinetic energy of a rolling object from the perspective of a stationary object, we should first isolate the aspect of the rolling that is pure rotation about an axis. The kinetic energy of this motion can be calculated: $K = \frac{1}{2}I_p\omega^2$. If we substitute the

parallel-axis theorem into this equation, we get: $K = \frac{1}{2}I_{cm}\omega^2 + \frac{1}{2}Mv_{cm}^2$. The first of the terms on the right side of the equation is the kinetic energy of the wheel associated with its rotation around an axis at the center of mass; the second term is the kinetic energy of the wheel associated with its translational motion.

Friction:

If a wheel is rolling at a constant speed, then the point at which it touches the ground will not slide, and there will be no friction. If, however, a force should act on the wheel, changing the speed of the center of mass or the angular speed of the wheel about the center, then the wheel may slide on the ground and be subject to friction. Until the wheel slides, the frictional force is static; once it slides, however, frictional force is kinetic. If a wheel is dropped onto an incline, the force of friction will actually propel it forward, as the sliding of the bottom of the wheel will encourage rotation. Indeed, when the rider of a bicycle pushes on the pedals to speed up, he or she is making use of the force of friction to accelerate.

Angular momentum

Linear momentum has an angular counterpart. If we imagine a particle moving with linear momentum p around an origin O, we can calculate the angular momentum: $\ell = r \times p = m(r \times v)$, in which r is the position vector of the particle with respect to O. In order to have an angular momentum, a particle need not rotate around the origin point. The SI unit for angular momentum is the kilogram-meter-squared per second. As with torque, angular momentum only has meaning when it is in reference to a stated origin. The direction of the angular momentum vector is always perpendicular to the plane formed by vectors r and p.

Newton's second law in angular form:
It seems that for every kind of linear motion, there is a counterpart in angular motion. The relation between torque and angular momentum is analogous to that between force and

linear momentum, and so we may rewrite Newton's second law (that is: $\sum F = \dfrac{dp}{dt}$) for

angular motion thus: $\sum \tau = \dfrac{d\ell}{dt}$. In words, we may say that the vector sum of all the torques

acting on a particle is equal to the time rate of change of the angular momentum of that

particle. Of course, the torque and linear momentum must be given in respect to the same

origin.

Angular momentum of a system of particles:

If we consider the motion of a system of particles, then the total angular momentum of this

system will be the vector sum of the individual momenta of all the particles:

$L = \ell_1 + \ell_2 + \ell_3 + ... + \ell_n = \displaystyle\sum_{i=1}^{n} \ell_i$. Some of the torques acting on the system will be internal,

meaning that they are forces exerted by one part of the system on another; these forces will

cancel one another out. External torques, those that are caused by forces outside the

system, can be calculated: $\sum \tau_{ext} = \dfrac{dL}{dt}$. This is Newton's second law as applied to a system of

particles and expressed in angular quantities. It states that the vector sum of the external

torques acting on a system of particles is equal to the time rate of change of the angular

momentum of that system.

Angular momentum of a rigid body:

If we consider a case in which a system of particles makes up a rigid body and rotates

around an axis, we may calculate angular momentum in the following way. First, let us say

that the body rotates around the z-axis and moves with angular speed ω. The angular

momentum of the body can be found by adding together all of the z-components of the

angular momenta of the mass elements of the body.

Conservation of angular momentum:

In order to derive the law of conservation of angular momentum, we must begin with

Newton's second law as it is arranged for angular motion: $\sum \tau_{ext} = \frac{dL}{dt}$. If there is no net

external torque acting on the system in question, then this equation will become $\frac{dL}{dt} = 0$, and

L will have become a constant. This assertion of the conservation of angular momentum

can be phrased thus: if no net external torque acts on a system, the vector angular

momentum L of that system remains constant, regardless of the changes that take place

within the system. As with the other conservation equations, this holds true even when we

look at motion outside the boundaries of Newtonian mechanics (that is, motion that occurs

at very high speeds or involves subatomic particles).

Equilibrium

We may say that an object is in a state of equilibrium when it has a constant linear

momentum P at its center of mass, and when angular momentum L is the also constant

around the center of mass. In other words, a wheel may be in equilibrium when it is

spinning at a constant speed, and a hockey puck may be in equilibrium as it slides across

ice. The phrase static equilibrium, however, is reserved for objects in which both linear

and angular momentum are at zero. An object sitting on a table could be considered as

being in static equilibrium. A body is said to be in stable static equilibrium when it would

be difficult to permanently remove from its state of poise; an unstable static equilibrium,

on the other hand, is very easily disturbed.

Requirements of equilibrium:

If a body is in translational equilibrium, then its linear momentum will be constant, and

there will be a perfect balance of forces: $\sum F_{ext} = 0$. Likewise, a body in rotational

equilibrium will have a constant angular momentum, and again there will be a balance of

torques: $\sum \tau_{ext} = 0$. Both of these equations are vector equations, and as such are equivalent

- 49 -

to three scalar equations for the three dimensions of motion. We may say that the two requirements for a body to be in equilibrium are that the vector sum of all the external forces acting on the body must be zero, and the vector sum of all the external torques acting on the body must also be zero.

Center of gravity

Although weight is generally accounted for as a force vector pointing to the center of the earth from a body's center of mass, it actually is a force affecting each part of the body individually. There may be situations in which it is necessary to determine whether g has the same influence on all parts of the body. If we examine an irregular body, we may find that its center of mass is not in the same place as its center of gravity: the point where the vector sum of all the weight forces of the atoms is said to act. If the body should be supported at its center of gravity, it will be in static equilibrium, and the force supporting it will me equal to the weight of the body.

Finding and evaluating:
In order to assess the center of gravity of a body, let us posit a body with its center of gravity at the origin of a coordinate system , and the rest of the body divided into sections Δm. If we place a force F' at O (the center of gravity), then the body will be in equilibrium provided F' equals mg, the weight of the body. In assessing the torques on the body, we will know that F' is exerting no torque, and therefore will be the center of mass (not of gravity, yet) assuming torques are balanced. If F' is applied at a center of mass which is not also a center of gravity, then the body will continue to rotate until it is moved to that point.

Elasticity

Uniform bodies are made up of large numbers of atoms which have come together and formed a solid structure. These atoms are held together by lattice-like inter-atomic forces. The degree to which these structures are strong or weak is known as the body's elasticity.

Every rigid body is elastic to some extent, meaning that their dimensions can be slightly altered through the application of force. The force undergone by a body is called stress: the deforming force per unit area. Strain is the term used technically to refer to the deformation of the body. Stress and strain are proportional to one another, and the constant of proportionality is known as the modulus of elasticity (stress = modulus x strain). A couple basic measures of elasticity seek to discover yield strength, the stress level at which an object is permanently deformed, and ultimate strength, the stress level at which the object ruptures.

Tension and compression:

Calculating simple tension or compression is easy: divide the force by the area over which it acts, assuming that force is perpendicular to area. Strain (or deformity) can then be measured as the change in length divided by the original length. The modulus of elasticity used for tensile and compressive stresses is called Young's modulus, represented E:

$\frac{F}{A} = E\frac{\Delta L}{L}$. Interestingly, although the modulus of elasticity may be the same for both tension and compression, ultimate strength can still be quite different for these two actions. One example of this phenomenon is concrete, which is very strong in compression but very weak in tension.

Shearing

Shearing is the kind of stress in which a solid body is deformed by a force that is applied along one of its sides. So, in these cases stress will also be measured as a force per unit area, even though the force vector will lie in the plane of the area rather than perpendicular to it. Strain, therefore, is a dimensionless ratio $\Delta x/L$, in which Δx is the distance away from its original position that the plane moves. The elasticity equation applied to shearing is written $\frac{F}{A} = G\frac{\Delta x}{L}$, in which G is the shearing modulus. Shearing stress is most commonly associated with bone fractures that occur due to bending.

Hydraulic compression

Hydraulic compression is the force exerted by a pressurized liquid on a solid object. Under intense pressure, a solid object may undergo a reduction in volume. Strain is typically measured as ΔV/V, the change in the object's volume divided by its original volume. The stress is the same as fluid pressure p on the object, and is again considered to be a force per unit measure. The equation for hydraulic compression is $p = B\dfrac{\Delta V}{V}$, in which B is the modulus of elasticity, known here as the bulk modulus. One common example of hydraulic pressure occurs at the bottom of the ocean, where steel compresses about .025%.

Simple harmonic motion

Harmonic motion, also known as periodic motion, is any motion that repeats itself at regular intervals. In order to analyze simple harmonic motion, let us imagine a system consisting of one particle moving back and forth across an origin of the x-axis. One important aspect of such motion is its frequency; that is, the rate at which oscillations are completed. The SI unit of frequency is the hertz, which is oscillations per second. Period, then, which is the time it takes to complete one oscillation, is found: $T = \dfrac{1}{f}$. For simple harmonic motion, we can find the displacement of the particle x from the origin with this formula: $x(t) = x_m \cos(\omega t + \phi)$. The phrase simple harmonic motion indicates that periodic motion is a sinusoidal function of time.

Equation for displacement:
Let us begin with the equation for displacement during simple harmonic motion: $x(t) = x_m \cos(\omega t + \phi)$. In this equation, x_m stands for amplitude: maximum displacement of the particle from the x-axis. The time-varying quantity $(\omega t + \phi)$ is referred to as the phase of the motion, and ϕ (the phase constant, or phase angle) depends on the magnitude of the displacement and the velocity of the particle. The constant ω can be calculated:

$\omega = \dfrac{2\pi}{T} = 2\pi f$. This quantity is known as the angular frequency of the motion, and it is expressed in radians per second.

Velocity:

To find the velocity of a particle moving with simple harmonic motion, we take the equation for the displacement of the particle ($x(t) = x_m \cos(\omega t + \phi)$) and differentiate with respect to time, giving us the equation: $v(t) = -\omega x_m \sin(\omega t + \phi)$. Just as the equation for displacement has a term expressing amplitude, the term ωx_m in this equation is called the velocity amplitude. That is to say, the velocity of the particle will vary depending on where it is in its oscillation. When the magnitude of the displacement is greatest, the magnitude of the velocity is least, and vice versa.

Acceleration:

In order to find the acceleration of an oscillating particle, we must start with the equation for velocity: $v(t) = -\omega x_m \sin(\omega t + \phi)$. Then, we simply differentiate for time once again, and arrive at: $a(t) = -\omega^2 x_m \cos(\omega t + \phi)$. The positive quantity $\omega^2 x_m$ is referred to as the acceleration amplitude (a_m). This equation can be combined with the equation for displacement in simple harmonic motion to create: $a(t) = -\omega^2 x(t)$. This equation expresses one of the characteristic qualities of simple harmonic motion: acceleration is proportional to displacement but opposite in sign. These two quantities are related by the square of the angular frequency, such that displacement is greatest where acceleration is least and vice versa.

Force law:

If we know the rate of acceleration of an oscillating particle, we can quickly use Newton's second law to find out what force must be acting on the particle. Indeed, we will quickly find that we are dealing with a familiar scenario in which force is proportional to displacement but opposite in sign: $F = -kx$, or Hooke's Law. Here, though, the spring

- 53 -

constant is $k = mw^2$. This is referred to as a linear simple harmonic oscillator, meaning that F is proportional to x rather than to some other power of x. The angular frequency of the simple harmonic motion is found: $\omega = \sqrt{\dfrac{k}{m}}$. The period of the linear oscillator can be found:

$T = 2\pi\sqrt{\dfrac{m}{k}}$.

Energy considerations:

Although the energy of a linear oscillator will be constantly changing from kinetic to potential and back again, the overall quantity of mechanical energy will remain the same. The potential energy of a linear oscillator is totally associated with the displacement capacity of the spring, and can be found: $U(t) = \dfrac{1}{2}kx^2 = \dfrac{1}{2}kx^2\cos^2(\omega t + \phi)$. The kinetic energy of the system is entirely associated with the block, and can be found: $K(t) = \dfrac{1}{2}mv^2 = \dfrac{1}{2}kx_m^2\sin^2$.

Mechanical energy is found with the equation $E = U + K = \dfrac{1}{2}kx_m^2$. This is a constant, and is independent of time.

Angular simple harmonic oscillator:

One common form of harmonic motion studied in physics is that of an angular simple harmonic oscillator. This consists of a circular weight suspended from a wire: when the weight is twisted, a tension is created in the wire. This device is known as a torsion (twisting) pendulum. If the pendulum weight is rotated through angle ϕ, the restoring torque will be: $\tau = -\kappa\theta$, in which κ is the torsion constant. This equation is the angular form of Hooke's law, and with a bit of replacement can be converted into an equation for the period of an angular simple harmonic oscillator: $T = 2\pi\sqrt{\dfrac{I}{\kappa}}$.

Uniform circular motion:

The astronomical observations made by Galileo led him to the insight that simple harmonic motion is simply the projection of uniform circular motion on a diameter of the circle in which the uniform circular motion occurs. In other words, simple harmonic motion is uniform circular motion viewed edge on. If, for instance, we look at a particle P' moving at a constant angular speed ω around a circle with radius x_m, we may say that the position of the particle is $\omega t + \phi$, in which ϕ is the original angular position. If we project this point onto an x-axis, then we may find the location as: $x(t) = x_m \cos(\omega t + \phi)$, the exact same equation used to find displacement during simple harmonic motion.

Pendulums

Simple pendulums:

Unlike an angular simple harmonic oscillator, which moves because of the elastic properties of a wire, a simple pendulum depends on the force of gravity for its motion. If we consider for instance a simple pendulum consisting of a mass hanging from an inelastic string without mass, then we may describe its restoring force after it is moved as: $F = -mg \sin \theta$, in which θ is the angle by which the mass is removed from its resting position. If the angle is very small, then $\sin \theta \approx \theta$, and the motion of the pendulum is like that of a simple harmonic oscillator. If this is the case, then the period of our simple pendulum can be found: $T = 2\pi \sqrt{\dfrac{L}{g}}$. Again, this only holds if the angular amplitude (θ_m) is very small.

Physical pendulums:

A physical pendulum is a more realistic version of a pendulum than the simple pendulum, consisting of a solid body that is suspended from some fixed point. We assume that a physical pendulum moves because of its weight, which acts on center of mass C. When the pendulum is moved to some point beyond its normal resting position, it has a restoring force: $\tau = -(mg \sin \theta)(h)$. As with the simple pendulum, we will find that the behavior of the pendulum is harmonic only when the amplitude of the displacement angle is quite small, in

which case the period may be found: $T = 2\pi\sqrt{\dfrac{I}{mgh}}$, in which I is the rotational inertia of the

pendulum and h is the distance between the point of support and the center of mass of a

swinging pendulum.

Finding the gravitational constant:

One of the most common and practical applications of physics is using a pendulum to

determine the rate of free-fall acceleration. If we assume our pendulum to be a uniform

rod of approximately length L, in which h is the distance between the suspension point and

the center of mass, and we know that the rotational inertia of such a pendulum will be

about $\dfrac{1}{2}mL^2$, then we can substitute and solve for g: $g = \dfrac{8\pi^2 L}{3T^2}$. In other words, by knowing

the length and period of a pendulum, we can determine the rate of free-fall acceleration.

Newton's law of gravitation

One of Newton's major insights into the behavior of physical objects was that every object

in the universe exerts an attractive force on every other body. In quantitative terms, we

may say that the gravitational force with which particles attract one another is: $F = G\dfrac{m_1 m_2}{r^2}$,

in which r is the distance between the particles and G is the gravitational constant.

Although this equation is usually applied to particles, it may also be applied to objects

assuming that they are small relative to the distance between them. Newton expressed this

relation by saying that a uniform spherical shell of matter attracts a particle that is outside

the shell as if all the matter were concentrated at the center. In the case of gravitation on

earth, for instance, objects behave as if the earth were a single particle located at its center,

and having the mass of the entire earth.

Gravitation

Principle of superposition:

Sometimes, finding the gravitational force among a group of particles is more complicated than simply using Newton's law of gravitation. In such cases, we may use what is known as the principle of superposition, which basically asserts that the net effect is the sum of the individual effects. This simply entails calculating the gravitational force acting on a certain particle by each other particle: $F_1 = F_{12} + F_{13} + F_{14} + ... + F_{1n}$. This equation can also be expressed:

$F_1 = \sum_{i=2}^{n} F_{1i}$, in which i is the index of all acting forces. In the case of the force of an extended object acting on a particle, we must divide the object up into differential units which exert a differential force, and our equation becomes: $F_1 = \int dF$, in which the integral is taken over the extended object.

Near the surface of the earth:

In order to begin considering the gravitational force near the surface of the earth, we should for the time being ignore the rotation of the earth and assume it is a uniform sphere. We can then say that the magnitude of the gravitational force acting on a particle is:

$F = G \dfrac{Mm}{r^2}$, in which M is the mass of the earth. When dropped, the particle will accelerate at a rate of a_g, which can be found: $a_g = \dfrac{GM}{r^2}$. This rate will be different at different altitudes around the world. Gravitational acceleration is different than the rate of free-fall acceleration.

Gravitational acceleration:

There are a few reasons why gravitational acceleration is not the same thing as the rate of free-fall acceleration. For one thing, the earth is not a uniform body. In fact, the density of the earth varies throughout its many layers, and the density of the crust (outermost layer) varies at different locations around the world. Another reason is that the earth is not a perfect sphere. On the contrary, it is flattened at the poles and bulging around the equator. Finally, the earth is constantly rotating. Its rotation axis runs through the north and south poles. This means that an object located anywhere on earth other than the poles will be rotating in a circle around the rotation axis, and will have a centripetal acceleration that points to the center of this circle. This centripetal acceleration will require a centripetal force also pointing to the center.

Measuring the gravitational constant G:

We can determine the value of the gravitational constant G by measuring the gravitational force between two bodies of known mass. The most common experiment achieving this goal is set up by fixing two small spheres with mass m at the ends of a rod suspended at its midpoint by a wire, and thus forming a torsion balance. Two large spheres, then, are place along the circle traversed by the small spheres when torsion is applied. The small balls will eventually settle into a position whereby their gravitational attraction to the larger balls is equal to the torque of the twisting wire. G can then be determined with the equation:

$G = \dfrac{\tau R^2}{MmL}$, in which L is the length of the rod.

Gravitation inside the earth:

Newton's shell theorem, appended to his law of gravitation, asserts that a uniform spherical shell of matter will exert a gravitational force on a particle outside of it as if all of the mass of the shell were concentrated at its center. This theorem also applies in situations in which the particle is located inside the shell. Namely, it states that a uniform shell of matter will exert no gravitational force on a particle located inside of it. This is not the case with the earth, because the outer crust is so much less dense than the inner that the gravitational force exerted on an object does not lessen as the object gets closer to the surface. In a uniform body, however, approaching the center would mean that there would be less and less of the body to exert gravitational pressure, and so the amount of gravitational pressure would decrease.

Gravitational potential energy:

In order to take a look at gravitational potential energy, let us imagine two masses, m and M, separated by a distance r. We might imagine m as a ball and M as the earth, although this scenario can apply to any other two masses. We will find that the gravitational potential energy can be found: $U(r) = -\dfrac{GMm}{r}$. As the distance between the two objects grows larger, the potential energy diminishes. It should be noted that the amount of potential energy cannot be ascribed to one or the other particle: it belongs to the system as a whole. If the system contain more than two particles, we must consider each pair of particles in turn and then add up the results.

Proof of gravitational potential energy:

If we were to drop a ball, we would find that the potential energy of the ball at a given point P in its descent is the negative of the work done by the gravitational force during its fall to this point. In equation form, we could calculate potential energy: $U = -W = -\int_{\infty}^{r} F(x)\,dx$. The vector of F(x) points toward the center of the earth, and the vector dx points in the opposite direction, so the angle between them is always 180 degrees. This allow us to simplify the equation until we arrive at: $U(r) = -\dfrac{GMm}{r}$. In each case, the amount of work performed is the negative of the change in potential energy between two points in the ball's descent.

Escape speed:

Using the basic equation for gravitational potential energy, $U(r) = -\dfrac{GMm}{r}$, we can determine the initial speed at which a projectile will need to be fired if it is to continue moving upward forever. This is known as the escape speed, and can be determined with the equation: $v = \sqrt{\dfrac{2GM}{R}}$, in which M is the mass of the Earth, and R is the radius of the Earth. This equation assumes that the total energy of the body while on the surface of the ground was zero. The escape speed for Earth is approximately 11 kilometers per second, whereas to escape the gravity of the moon, a much smaller body, an object need only attain a speed of 2.38 kilometers per second.

Kepler's Laws for planets and satellites

Law of orbits:

Kepler's first law describing the movement of planets states that all planets move in elliptical orbits, with the sun at one focus. If we are to consider the motion of one planet around the sum, we will assume that its mass is much smaller than that of the sun, such that the center of mass of the system is almost in the middle of the sun. The orbit of the planet will then be defined by the semimajor axis a (that is, half the length of the ellipse) and the eccentricity e (the degree to which the orbit is not circular). The orbits of the planets are only very slightly elliptical, thought they are often exaggerated on diagrams. In a planetary orbit, ea is the distance from the center of the ellipse to either focus.

Laws of areas and periods:

Kepler's second law for planets and satellites states that any line that connects a planet to the sun will sweep out equal areas in equal times. In other words, the planet will move most slowly when it is far away from the sum, and fastest when it is closest. This law is basically the same thing as the law of conservation of angular momentum. Kepler's third law for planets states that the square of the period of any planet is proportional to the cube of the semimajor axis of its orbit. This relation can be expressed: $T^2 = \left(\dfrac{4\pi^2}{GM}\right) r^3$. The quantity in parentheses in this equation is a constant, its only variable being the mass of the central body. This equation holds up for elliptical orbits as well.

Fluids

It sounds obvious, perhaps, but fluids can best be defined as substances that flow. A fluid will conform, slowly or quickly, to any container in which it is placed. This is because a fluid is unable to maintain a force tangential to its surface. In other words, fluids cannot withstand shearing stress. They can, on the other hand, exert a force perpendicular to their surface. Both liquids and gases are considered to be fluids. Fluids, essentially, are those substance in which the atoms are not arranged in any permanent, rigid way. In ice, for instance, atoms are all lined up in what is known as a crystalline lattice, while in water and steam the only intermolecular arrangements are haphazard connections between neighboring molecules.

Fluid density:

The density of a fluid is generally expressed with the symbol ρ. In order to find the density of a particular fluid, we generally isolate a small volume of the fluid and determine its mass. Then, the density may be found with the simple equation: $\rho = \frac{\Delta m}{\Delta V}$. It is generally assumed that the volume will never be measured at an amount so small as to have an inordinate number of atoms, and so the density of the fluid will be the same everywhere. Density is a scalar property, meaning that it has no direction component. It is typically measured in SI units of kilograms per cubic meter. While the density of a gas will tend to fluctuate considerably depending on the level of pressure, the density of a liquid is comparatively stable.

Fluid pressure:

In the case of fluids, pressure is typically measured by placing a small, spring-mounted sensor inside the fluid and measuring the degree to which the spring is compressed. Quantitatively, the pressure of the fluid is calculated: $p = \frac{\Delta F}{\Delta A}$. Experiment has shown that the pressure will be the same no matter in which direction in the fluid the sensor is placed. Pressure, like fluid density, is a scalar, and does not have a direction. This is true even though the force compressing the spring of the sensor has a direction. The equation for pressure is concerned only with the magnitude of that force, not with the direction in which it is pointing. The SI unit of pressure is the Newton per square meter, or pascal.

Fluids at rest:

As every deep-sea diver knows, the pressure of water becomes greater the deeper you go below the surface; conversely, experienced mountain climbers know that air pressure decreases as they gain a higher altitude. These pressures are typically referred to as hydrostatic pressures, because they involve fluids at rest. If we wanted to find the pressure of water at a distance h below the surface, then we could use this equation: $p = p_0 + \rho g h$, in which p_0 is the pressure at the surface of the water. The final term of this equation, $\rho g h$, is often referred to as gauge pressure: the difference between the pressure at a certain depth and atmospheric pressure. The pressure at a given depth depends only on the depth, and not on any horizontal factors.

Atmospheric pressure

A mercury barometer is the most common way to measure the pressure of the atmosphere. It is constructed by filling a long glass tube with mercury and inverting it such that its open end is face-down in a dish of mercury. The top of the tube will contain mercury vapor, a fluid with an extremely small pressure. This instrument is then placed into the environment we seek to investigate, and we can look at the height attained by the mercury liquid to determine the pressure of the external environment. This can be done with this equation: $p_0 = \rho g h$, in which h is the height of the mercury liquid. Of course, this measure depends on a constant reading for g, so it can only be performed in areas where the gravitational constant is known to be standard.

Pascal's principle

Anytime you squeeze a tube of toothpaste, you are demonstrating the idea known as Pascal's principle. This principle states that a change in the pressure applied to an enclosed fluid is transmitted undiminished to every portion of the fluid as well as to the walls of the containing vessel. If, for instance, we had a container filled with liquid, on top of which a piston rests, loaded down with a lead weight. The atmosphere, container, lead weight, and piston will all be exerting pressure p_{ext} on the liquid, and so the total pressure on the liquid will be: $p = p_{ext} + \rho g h$. If we added another weight to the piston, however, we would be increasing p_{ext} without in any way affecting the height of the liquid in the container. Since this is so, the pressure change will hold for all points within the liquid, as Pascal's principle suggests.

Archimedes' principle

If an object is submerged in water, it will have a buoyant force exerted on it in the upward direction. This force is caused by the difference in water pressure depending on depth: the object will naturally be propelled upward by the greater pressure at its bottom. Often, of course, this buoyant force is much too small to keep an object from sinking to the bottom. This buoyant force is one of the reasons why it is easier to lift heavy objects when they are underwater. This idea of buoyancy is summarized in Archimedes' principle; a body wholly or partially submerged in a fluid will be buoyed up by a force equal to the weight of the fluid that the body displaces. A piece of wood floating on top of the water, for instance, will displace less water since it breaks the plane of the surface.

Equilibrium of floating objects:
Even though the weight of a floating object is precisely balanced by a buoyant force, these forces will not necessarily act at the same point. The weight will act from the center of mass of the object, while the buoyancy will act from the center of mass of the hole in the water made by the object (known as the center of buoyancy). If the floating object is tilted,

then the center of buoyancy will shift and the object may be unstable. In order to remain in equilibrium, the center of buoyancy must always shift in such a way that the buoyant force and weight provide a restoring torque, one that will restore the body to its upright position. This concept is of course crucial to the construction of boats which must always be made to encourage restoring torque.

Ideal fluids in motion

Since the motion of actual fluids is extremely complex, physicists usually refer to ideal fluids when they make their calculations. Using ideal fluids in equations is a bit like discounting friction in other calculations; it tends to make the process mathematically manageable. So, when we deal with ideal fluids, we are making four assumptions. First, we are assuming that the flow is steady; in other words, the velocity of every part of the fluid is the same. We also assume that fluids are incompressible, and therefore have a consistent density. We assume that fluids are nonviscous, meaning that they flow easily and without resistance. Finally, we assume that the flow of ideal fluids is irrotational: that is, it particles in the fluid will not rotate around a center of mass.

Streamlines

A streamline is the path traced out by a very small unit of fluid, which we will refer to as a particle. Although the velocity of a particle may change in both magnitude and direction, streamlines will never cross one another. In many instances of flow, several streamlines will group together to form what is called a tube of flow. If we were to make two cross-sections of a tube of flow, A_1 and A_2, then we would find that since fluid is incompressible, the same amount of fluid passes through the two cross-sections over the same interval of time. This is expressed by the equation: $R = Av$, a constant, in which R is known as the volume flow rate. This equation is known as the equation of continuity; it suggests that flow will be faster in areas of the tube that are narrower.

Bernoulli's equation

Let us imagine a tube of flow. In time interval Δt, a volume of fluid ΔV enters the tube, as an equal amount exits at the other end. If we assume y, v, and p as the elevation, speed, and pressure of the fluid, then we may apply the law of conservation of energy:

$p_1 + \frac{1}{2}\rho v_i^2 + \rho g y_1 = p_2 + \frac{1}{2}\rho v_2^2 + \rho g y_2$. This equation, which can be rewritten $p + \frac{1}{2}\rho v^2 + \rho g y =$ to find a constant, is called Bernoulli's equation. It is essentially just a reformulation of the law of conservation of mechanical energy for fluid mechanics. One consequence of Bernoulli's equation is that if the elevation of the fluid remains constant, and the speed of a fluid particle increases as it travels along a streamline, the pressure will decrease. If the fluid slows down, the pressure will increase.

There are a few common situations that demonstrate the relations asserted by Bernoulli's equation. For one thing, we might consider the case of a high wind blowing past a house. If the wind is strong enough, the pressure outside the window will be so much smaller than the pressure inside that the window will break outward. When hurricanes tear the flat roofs off of buildings, Bernoulli's principle is at work. Also, if we consider a case in which someone has punctured a hole in a tank of liquid, we can rearrange Bernoulli's equation to find the velocity at which water is leaving the tank: $v = \sqrt{2gh}$. This velocity will be the same as if the water had been dropped from the top surface of the water to the point at which the hole was made.

Airplane wings:
Airplane wings are designed to take advantage of Bernoulli's principle so that an extremely heavy body can be lifted into the air. As the plane moves forward, air is forced down by the upward tilt of the wing, which is set at what is called the "attack angle." As the wing exerts a force on the airstream, so does the airstream push up on the wing, with a force that is called lift. Airplane wings are designed so that the streamlines will be wider below than above the wing, and so there is greater air pressure underneath the wing than above. This

is consistent with the fact that there is an upward force acting on the wing. The speed of the air will be considerably smaller below the wing than above, as the air is deflected by the wing with a force known as induced drag.

Electromagnetism

Electromagnetism is the combination of electrical and magnetic phenomena. Although we may assume that only things like power cords and home appliances utilize electricity, there is in actuality a great amount of electrical charge in every object we see and touch. One reason why this fact is not immediately apparent is because, in most objects, the amounts of positive and negative charge are equal and balanced. If the two types of charge are not balanced, however, there will be a net charge that can affect other objects. Therefore, when we say that an object is charged, what we really mean is that it is not neutral, that it has an unbalanced electrical charge. Charge imbalances are always small compared to the total amount of positive and negative charges in the object.

Electrical force

When objects possess an electrical charge (that is, when the positive and negative charges are imbalanced), they will exert a force on one another. The basic relation of electrical forces is that like charges will repel one another, while unlike charges will attract one another. The words "positive" and "negative" that are used to describe electrical charge are arbitrary; they were introduced by Benjamin Franklin as a simple way to classify charge, and not because of any innate characteristic of one or the other charge. This basic principle of attraction and repulsion is expressed quantitatively in Coulomb's law of electrostatic force, in which the word electrostatic means that the charges are either stationary or moving very slowly in relation to one another.

Conductors and insulators

In many materials, a negative charge can move freely; these materials are known as conductors, and include metals and the human body. Other materials inhibit the movement of charge and are known as insulators. Glass, pure water, and plastic are all insulators. There are a couple of different ways to neutralize the effects of an electrical charge. When we create a pathway whereby charge can move to the earth's surface, we are said to be grounding the object. When we neutralize the charge of an object by eliminating the charge imbalance, we are said to be discharging the objects. Charge is altered by changes in the number of electrons in the atoms of a material. Since electrons are negatively charged, a positive charge is caused by a deficiency of electrons, while a negative charge is caused by an abundance of electrons.

Semiconductors and superconductors:
Semiconductors, as the name suggests, are materials that only partially conduct electrical charge. The elements silicon and germanium are both semiconductors, and are frequently used in microelectronic devices for this reason. Superconductors are those materials that in no way inhibit the flow of electricity. Most conductors put up a small bit of resistance to the flow of electrical current, but in a superconductor the resistance is exactly zero. A current introduced to a superconducting ring, for instance, will flow forever. For a long time, superconductors were rarely used because they required the conducting material to be cooled to a freezing temperature. Recent innovations, however, have allowed scientists to create superconductors at much higher temperatures.

Coulomb's law

If two particles have charge magnitudes q_1 and q_2, and are separated by distance r, then the electrostatic force of attraction or repulsion between them can be calculated: $F = k\dfrac{q_1 q_2}{r^2}$, in which k is a constant. This is known as Coulomb's law. We should note the similarity to

- 67 -

Newton's equation for the magnitude of the gravitational force between two

particles: $F = G\dfrac{m_1 m_2}{r^2}$. The main difference between the equations is that while electrical force may be attractive or repulsive, gravitational force is only attractive. No experiment has ever contradicted Coulomb's law, even those conducted at the subatomic level. The constant k in the equation is called the electrostatic constant.

Coulomb:

The SI unit for charge is the coulomb. One coulomb is the amount of charge transferred through the cross section of a wire in one second when the wire contains one ampere of current. Oftentimes, the electrostatic constant in Coulomb's law will be written $1/4\pi\epsilon_0$,

making the equation: $F = \dfrac{1}{4\pi\epsilon_0}\dfrac{q_1 q_2}{r^2}$. This is done because it will simplify many more complex equations. The quantity ϵ_0 is called the permittivity constant, and is calculated: $\epsilon_0 = 8.85\times10^{-12}\, C^2/N\square m^2$. As with gravitational force, electrostatic force obeys the law of superposition: the net force of a number of charged particles on a single particle is simply the vector sum of those individual forces.

Shell theorems and spherical conductors:

Coulomb's law for electrostatics will obey the shell theorems developed to describe gravitational forces. In other words, a shell of uniform charge attracts or repels a charged particle that is outside the shell as if all of the shell's charge were concentrated at its center. Also, a shell of uniform charge will exert no electrostatic force on a charged particle that is located inside of it. In the case of spherical conductors, an excess charge placed on the outside of the sphere will spread evenly over the external surface of the sphere. Specifically, a group of excess electrons placed on the outside of a metal sphere will move apart until they are spread uniformly over the entire surface of the sphere.

Quantized charge

For a long time, scientists thought that electricity was a continuous fluid, all of the same charge. However, advances in both the study of fluids and of electricity have revealed that electrical charge, like air or water, is actually a collection of many discrete units of multiples of a certain elementary charge. Specifically, the elementary charge e has the value: $e = 1.60 \times 10^{-19} C$. The net charge q of an object, then, can be written: $q = ne$, $n = \pm 1, \pm 2, \pm 3, \cdots$. When we say that electrical charge can only have a collection of discrete values, rather than one uniform value, we are saying that charge is quantized.

Conservation of charge

When we say that an electrical charge has been created, we do not mean that any electrons have been created or destroyed. Rather, we mean simply that the balance of electrons in an object has changed, creating a net positive or negative charge. Benjamin Franklin was the first to assert this hypothesis regarding the conservation of charge, and it has held for all subsequent experimentation. Even during the process of radioactive decay, in which a nucleus spontaneously transforms itself, overall charge is conserved. Charge conservation also occurs during the process of annihilation, in which an electron and its antiparticle, the positron, combine to form a pair of chargeless gamma rays.

Electric field

Scientists were for a long time puzzled as to how electrically charged particles could exert force on one another without ever touching. To resolve this problem, they have developed the idea of the electrical field: an area within which a charged object will be able to exert a force on other objects. Electric field is similar to temperature field; just as the temperature of the room in which you are sitting will have a definite value at any specific point, so will the electrical force created by an object be able to be determined at any particular location in its electric field. Unlike a temperature field, however, an electric field is a vector field.

Indeed, an electric field is composed of the distribution of vectors, one for each point in the region around a charged object.

Electric field equation:

In order to define a particular electric field, we may place an object with positive charge q_0 (called a test charge) somewhere near the charged particle, and then measure the force exerted on the object. We may then say that electric field E at that point is: $E = \dfrac{F}{q_0}$. Electric field is a vector, and the direction of E will be the direction of the force acting on the test charge. If we want to fully define some region of an electric field, we must find measures for electric field at every point within that region. The SI unit for electric filed is the Newton per coulomb. When performing this operation, we will assume that the presence of the test charge does not affect in any way the charge distribution of the electric field.

Electric field lines:

Physicists generally use electric field lines to make it easier for them to visualize the pattern of a particular electric field. At any point, the direction of a straight field line (or the direction of the tangent to a curved field line) gives the direction of the electric field at that point. Also, field lines are drawn so that the number of lines per unit area is proportional to the magnitude of the electric field; this explains why the lines are usually at their most dense around the charged object. Another property of electric field lines is that they always extend away from positive charge and towards negative charge. One common pattern created by electric field lines occurs in an electric field containing two objects containing opposite charge of the same magnitude; in this arrangement, known as an electric dipole, field lines extend out from each body in the direction of the other body.

Point charge:

In order to determine the value of the electric field due to a point charge (a charged particle), we place a test charge at some point distance r from the point charge. Using Coulomb's law, we may then determine the magnitude of the electrostatic force acting on that test charge. The direction of the force will be directly away from the point charge if the charge is positive, and directly toward the charge if it is negative. We can then determine the magnitude of the electric file vector as: $E = \dfrac{F}{q_0} = \dfrac{1}{4\pi \in_0} \dfrac{q}{r^2}$. The direction of E will be the same as that on the test charge. In cases where more than one point charge is acting on the test charge, we can determine the net or resultant electric field by adding up the charges.

Electric dipole:

If two particles are configured in an electric dipole (that is, they have charges of equal but opposite magnitude), we may want to determine the value of the electric field at point P distance z from the midpoint of the dipole on its central axis. We assume that this axis will contain the electric fields of the two charged particles, as well as the combined field.

For point P , we can calculate the electric field as: $E = \dfrac{1}{2\pi \in_0} \dfrac{p}{z^3}$, in which $p = qd$, what is known as the dipole moment. The electric dipole moment is a vector that has its direction from the negative to the positive end of the dipole.

Line of charge:

When we deal with a huge number of point charges spread out over a line, surface, or volume, then we assume we are dealing with a continuous rather than a discrete distribution. Since there can be billions of point charges responsible for a uniform charge, we will find it easier to use calculus than to calculate the field individually. Moreover, we will usually express the charge in terms of a charge density, rather than as a total charge. In the case of a line of charge, for instance, we will determine the linear charge density λ, expressed in the SI unit coulomb per meter. Other charge densities include surface charge density (σ), measured in coulomb per meters squared; and volume charge density (ρ), measure in coulomb per meters cubed.

Charged ring:

Let us imagine a charged ring with radius R and uniform positive linear charge density λ. We want to determine the electric field at point P, a distance z from the plane of the ring along its central axis. Obviously, we cannot treat the charge created by the ring as if it were a point charge. Instead, we have to divide the ring into differential elements of charge that can be measured and combined to calculate the net charge. For each differential element, the charge will be: $dq = \lambda ds$. If we then establish the electric field at P and assume that all of the perpendicular elements of this filed will cancel one another out, we are left with the parallel elements, which may be calculated: $E = \dfrac{qz}{4\pi \in_0 (z^2 + R^2)^{3/2}}$. If the charge on the ring were negative rather than positive, we would simply reverse the direction of the vector for the electric field.

Charged disk:

Let us imagine a charged disk of radius R with a positive surface charge of uniform density σ. We want to find the electric field at point P, which is distance z from the disk along its central axis. The easiest way to determine this field is to treat the disk as a collection of concentric rings. We may then find the electric fields for each of these rings and integrate these to find the field for the disk. Using our equation for finding the electric field of a ring, $E = \dfrac{qz}{4\pi \in_0 (z^2 + R^2)^{3/2}}$, we may integrate and arrive at: $E = \dfrac{\sigma}{2 \in_0}\left(1 - \dfrac{z}{\sqrt{z^2 + R^2}}\right)$. If we imagine the radius of the disk expanding towards infinity, while the distance z is remaining finite, the part of this equation in parentheses will approach zero, and we will have the equation for a charged sheet of infinite area: $E = \dfrac{\sigma}{2 \in_0}$.

Point charge in an electric field:

Instead of always determining the electric field created by a charged particle, physicists sometimes need to determine the effects on a charged particle of moving into an elaready established electric field. When this happens, an electrostatic force acts on the particle; this vector can be found: $F = qE$, where q is the charge of the particle and E is the electric field into which it has moved. Many of the equations for charge are scalar equations and therefore only express magnitude; this is not one of those equations. The directions for F and E will be the same if q is positive, and in opposite directions if q is negative.

Dipole in an electric field:

When we are dealing with electric dipoles, we consider the electric dipole moment p to be a vector whose direction is along the dipole axis, pointing from the negative to the positive charge. We will see that the behavior of a dipole in a pre-existing electric field can be described entirely in terms of E and p, without any description of the structure of the dipole. Let us imagine a basic dipole in an electric field, with the angle θ between the dipole moment p and E. The forces on the two ends of the dipole will cancel each other out, but they will exert a net torque on the dipole about its center of mass, midway in betwen the charged ends. The equation for thi torque can be determined: $\tau = p \times E$. The torque on the dipole will always tend to rotate p in the direction of E.

Potential energy of an electric dipole:

There is a certain amount of potential energy associated with the presence of an electric dipole in an electric field. When dipole moment p is lined up with E (that is, when the dipole is in its equilibrium position), the dipole will have its smallest potential energy. The easiest way to determine the potential energy of the dipole is to imagine it perpendicular to E, and then, using the simple equation $U = -W$, we can find the potential energy at any particular angle by finding the amount of work it would take to move the dipole to that angle. This sequence then runs: $U = -W = -\int_{90°}^{\theta} \tau d\theta = \int_{90°}^{\theta} pE \sin\theta d\theta$, $U = -pE\cos\theta$, and is generalized in vector form as: $U = -p \Box E$.

Microwave cooking:

When a microwave oven is turned on, it creates a rapidly oscillating field of waves. When an object containing water is in the oven, this oscillating field exerts major torques on all of

- 73 -

the water molecules, forcing them to rotate back and forth in order to stay in alignment with their molecular dipoles. The electric field generated by the microwave causes the molecules to split apart from one another, move around, and join up with other molecules. The energy that they have to spare is converted into thermal energy, increasing the temperature of the water and thereby of the food. So, the operation of microwaves depends on the fact that water molecules are electric dipoles, and therefore can be moved by a shifting electric field.

Coulomb's law versus Gauss' law

Evaluating electrostatics becomes much simpler when the charged object in question is symmetrical. In such cases, we will find it easier to use Gauss' law than Coulomb's law. This is not to say that Coulomb's law is inapplicable to situations involving symmetrical objects; in fact, Coulomb's law can be used for every situation in electrostatics. Indeed, in situations where there is very little or no symmetry, Coulomb's law is the only way to determine electric field, and so elaborate calculations must be made using computers or calculus. Gauss' law, on the other hand, can simplify our calculations when symmetry exists, and can also yield some important insights not as fully exposed by Coulomb's law.

Coulomb's law as derived from Gauss' law:
Our goal here is to derive Coulomb's law from Gauss' law, and thereby prove that they are equivalent. Let us begin with a positive point charge q, inside a concentric spherical Gaussian surface of radius r. We will then divide this surface into differential areas dA. Because of the symmetry involved, we know that the electric field E will be perpendicular to the surface and directed outward from the interior. Since the angle between E and dA is zero, Gauss' law can be rewritten: $\epsilon_0 \oint E \cdot dA = \epsilon_0 \oint E dA = q$. E is a constant in the integration and can be brought in front of the integral: $\epsilon_0 E \oint dA = q$. The integral is now just the sum of

all the differential areas on the sphere and thus is just surface area, $4\pi r^2$. Substituting this,

we get: $E = \dfrac{1}{4\pi\epsilon_0}\dfrac{q}{r^2}$, the electric field due to a point charge as found using Coulomb's law.

Gaussian surface:

In order to apply Gauss' law, we must first understand the hypothetical closed surface known as the Gaussian surface. This surface may be of any shape at all, although most of the time physicists will select one that is in a similar shape as the one involved in their problem. When we say that it is a closed surface, we mean that it encloses a volume: cylinders and rectangular prisms are both shapes that could be used as Gaussian surfaces. Gauss' law will be able to relate the electric fields experienced on the Gaussian surface as well as those charges experienced inside the Gaussian surface. In other words, is we imagine a spherical Gaussian surface, with a uniform electric field directed outward at every point, we can assume that there is some net positive charge inside the sphere.

Flux

The word flux is derived from the Latin word meaning "to flow." Flux can be calculated for any vector field. Say, for instance, we send an airstream through a square of area A. We will use the symbol Φ for volume flow rate, or the amount of air that flows through the square in a given time interval. This rate will depend on the angle between the velocity of the air and the plane of the square: $\Phi = (v\cos\theta)A$. This rate of flow is a flux. If we want to rewrite this equation in terms of vectors, we have to make area vector A vector with magnitude equal to the area A and with direction normal to the plane of the area. We can then write our equation: $\Phi = vA\cos\theta = v\Box A$. We could then define Φ as the flux of the velocity field through the loop. This same calculation can be applied to electric fields.

Flux of the electric field:

In order to define the flux of the electric field, we imagine a Gaussian surface of any shape immersed in a nonuniform electric field, and then divide the surface into squares small

- 75 -

enough that we may imagine them to be flat. Once we have done this, we can use the simple equation for flux: $\Phi = \sum E \cdot \Delta A$. The sign resulting from the scalar product will determine whether the flux is positive, negative, or zero (if the flux points inward, it will be negative; outward, positive; on the surface, zero). An exact definition of flux can be determined by diminishing the area of the squares, such that the sum of the above equation becomes an integral: $\Phi = \oint E \cdot dA$.

Gauss' law:

In Gauss' law, the total flux Φ of an electric field through a closed surface is related to the net charge q enclosed by that surface. It is written: $\epsilon_0 \Phi = q$, where ϵ_0 is the permittivity constant, $8.85 \times 10^{-12} C^2 / N \cdot m^2$. If we substitute in the definition of flux, we can also write this equation: $\epsilon_0 \oint E \cdot dA = q$. In both these equations, net charge q is the algebraic sum of all the enclosed positive and negative charges. Any charge outside of the surface is not included in q. Also, the form or location of the charges inside the Gaussian surface is irrelevant.

Charged isolated conductor

One of the insights that we may glean from Gauss' law is that if an excess charge is placed on an isolated conductor, the charge will move entirely to the surface of the conductor. In other words, none of the excess charge will be found inside the conductor. His makes sense if we remember that like charges will repel one another; the surface of the conductor is as far away from one another as the constituents of the charge can get. A conductor, once charged, will develop an internal electric field. However, this electric field will quickly distribute itself such that the internal electric field is zero, the movement of charge is zero, and the net force on each charge is zero. This state is known as electrostatic equilibrium.

Isolated conductor with cavity:

Let us imagine a conductor hanging by an insulating string, so that it is entirely isolated, and then imagine that conductor having a cavity all the way through itself. We might wonder whether removing the material to form this cavity will affect the distribution of charge or the pattern of the electric field. If we were to draw a Gaussian surface around the cavity, but within the conducting body we will find that since there is no net electric field through the conductor, there can be no flux through this Gaussian surface. This means, according to Gauss' law, there can be no net charge enclosed within the new Gaussian surface. We must therefore assume that there is no charge on the walls of the cavity, and that the charge has remained on the outer surface of the conductor.

Isolated conductor:

Gauss' law asserts that once equilibrium has been established, any excess charge placed on an isolated conductor will be found to lie entirely on its surface. This will be true even when the conductor has an empty internal cavity. This fact (specifically, that E=0) will also prove that any excess charge placed on an isolated conductor will distribute itself on the surface of that conductor such that all points of the conductor, whether they are on the inside or the outside, will arrive at the same potential. Again, this will hold true regardless of whether the conductor has an internal cavity. Even if an isolated conductor is placed in an external electric field, all of the points of the conductor will still come to a single potential, because the free conduction electrons will be distributed such that the internal electric field cancels out the external electric field that would be there otherwise.

External electric field:

Although Gauss' law shows us that all excess charge on an isolated conductor will move to the surface of the conductor, unless that conductor is spherical the charge will not distribute itself uniformly. This variation can make it very difficult to determine the electric field set up by the surface charges. Using Gauss' law, however, it can be quite easy to determine the electric field just outside the surface of the conductor. All we need to do is take a small square of area, and imagine a Gaussian cylinder halfway inside the conductor and halfway outside, perpendicular to the surface. When we sum the flux of these Gaussian surfaces, we know the only flux will occur through the end of the cylinder outside the surface. We can then tally these measures to arrive at: $E = \dfrac{\sigma}{\epsilon_0}$. The magnitude of the electric field just outside the surface of a conductor will be proportional to the surface charge density at that location on the conductor.

Symmetry

Cylindrical symmetry:

Assuming that we have a section of charged cylindrical rod with a uniform linear charge density λ, we can use Gauss' law to find the magnitude of the electric field E at a distance r from the axis of the rod. We will use a cylindrical Gaussian surface, with radius r and length h. Since a cylinder is symmetric along every axis but its radial axis, we can assume that E will be uniform. The area of the cylindrical surface is $2\pi r h$. The flux of E through this body will therefore be $E A \cos\theta = E(2\pi r h)$. There will be no flux through the end caps, since E lies parallel to them at every point. We will find that electric field can be calculated: $E = \dfrac{\lambda}{2\pi \epsilon_0 \, r}$. This is the electric field caused by an infinitely long straight line of charge, at a point radial distance r from the line of charge.

Planar symmetry:

If we have a portion of insulating sheet with a charge of uniform surface charge density σ, we can use Gauss' law to find the electric field E a distance r in front of the sheet. In order to do so, let us imagine a cylindrical Gaussian surface extending through the sheet at a perpendicular angle. We know that E will be perpendicular to the sheet, and therefore perpendicular to the end caps as well. Since the electric field lines will only pierce the end caps, then, we can convert Gauss' law to $E = \dfrac{\sigma}{2\epsilon_0}$. Since the sheet is said to have uniform charge density, this measure will hold for any point a finite distance from the sheet.

If we imagine a cross section of thin, infinite conducting plate with an excess positive charge, we can use Gauss' law to determine the nature of the field it will create. If there is no external electric field, for instance, then the charge will simply spread out along the two faces of the plate with a uniform surface charge density σ_1. If we imagine two plates with identical magnitude of charge, one positive and one negative, and we arrange them parallel to one another, then the excess charge on both plates will move onto the inner face of the plates, and the electric field on the outside of the plates will be zero. In this scenario, we can find the magnitude of the electric field between the two plates as $E = \dfrac{2\sigma_1}{\epsilon_0} = \dfrac{\sigma}{\epsilon_0}$.

Spherical symmetry:

Gauss' law can be used to prove the two shell theorems of electric charge: namely, that a shell of uniform charge will act on a charged particle outside the shell as if all the charge were concentrated at the shell's center, and a shell of uniform charge will exert no electrostatic force on a charged particle inside the shell. If we imagine a spherical shell with total charge q, radius R, and two Gaussian surfaces s_1 and s_2, then we can say that for s_2, if $r \geq R$, then $E = \dfrac{1}{4\pi\epsilon_0}\dfrac{q}{r^2}$. In other words, the same field is created as would be created by a point charge q at the center of the charged shell. If we apply Gauss' law to s_1, in which $r \prec R$, then $E = 0$, because this Gaussian surface will enclose no charge.

Gravitation and electrostatics

Since Newton's law of gravitation and Coulomb's law of electrostatics are mathematically identical (both are inverse square laws), anything that can be deduced about gravitation can also be deduced about electrostatics. For instance, if we have a test particle with charge q_0 in an electric field, we can analyze its potential energy in the same way that we could analyze the potential energy of a particle with mass m_0 in free fall. The electric potential energy of a particle will depend on the position of that charge in the electric field. We will find that the change in the electric potential energy of a particle when it is moved in an electric field is the negative of the work done by the electrostatic force during is motion: $U = -W_{\infty f}$.

Potential difference

The potential energy of a point charge in an electric field will depend on the magnitude of the charge as well as the nature of the field. However, potential energy per unit charge V will have a unique value for any point in an electric field. This measure, which can be expressed U / q_0, will be independent of the magnitude of the test charge: it is only dependent on the electric field. So, the potential difference between any two place in an electric field will be equal to the difference in potential energy between the two points:

$\Delta V = V_f - V_i = \dfrac{W_{if}}{q_0}$. The work performed can be positive, negative, or zero. In a similar way, the minus sign in the equation will suggests that the final potential can be less than, equal to, or greater than the initial potential.

Electric potential:

When we know the potential difference ΔV between any two points, we will also know that the work we do to move the particle from one of the points to the other will be $q_0 \Delta V$, since the work we do is the negative of the work done by the field during this motion. If potential energy is zero at infinity, then potential must also be zero at infinity, and the potential at

any point in an electric field can be defined: $V = -\dfrac{W_{\infty f}}{q_0}$, where $W_{\infty f}$ is the work done by the electric field on the test charge as the charge moves from infinity to the point in question. This equation indicates that potential due to an isolated positive charge will be positive, and potential due to an isolated negative charge will be negative.

Electric potential energy vs. electric potential:

Though they have similar names, electric potential and electric potential energy are different quantities. Electric potential energy is the energy of a charged object in an external electric field. Electric potential energy is measured in joules. Electric potential, on the other hand, is a property of an electric field. It exists regardless of whether a charged object has been placed in the field, and is measured in joules per coulomb, or volts. The volt is a familiar measure to most people, though they may not know that it is a measure of potential difference. When the two ends of a voltmeter are touched to two different spots on an electric circuit, it is the potential difference that is being measured.

Equipotential surfaces:

Any group of points in space that have the same potential is called an equipotential surface. Oftentimes, physicists will use a series of equipotential surfaces rather than electric field lines to describe an electric field through a particular region. No net work will be done on a particle if it simply moves from one point to another on the same equipotential surface. If we are dealing with a point charge or a spherically symmetrical charge distribution, then we will find that our equipotential surfaces are concentric spheres. Equipotential surfaces will always be perpendicular to field lines and to E. If this were not the case, then E would have a component lying along the equipotential surface, which would mean that work was being done on a particle moving along with that component. This would make no sense, since no work can be done on a particle moving within an equipotential surface.

Calculating potential from field:

As long as we know the field vector E along every point of the path between two points, we can calculate the potential difference between those two points. By adding up all of the differential work done for each of the displacements between the two points, and the substituting potential difference for work, we will find: $V_f - V_i = -\int_i^f E \cdot ds$. If we know the electric field for an entire region, then we can calculate the difference in potential between any two points: $V = -\int_i^f E \, ds$. This equation gives us the potential V between any point f relative to zero potential at i.

Potential due to point charge:

Let us imagine an isolated positive point charge q, and then try to find the potential V due to q at P, a point radial distance r from the charge. In order to do so, we will imagine that test charge q_0 moves from infinity to P via a radial line. A bit of calculation will give us the equation for positive or negative point charge q: $V = \frac{1}{4\pi\epsilon_0}\frac{q}{r}$. In this equation, the sign for q can be either positive or negative, meaning that it does not just stand for the magnitude of the charge. In this equation, the sign of V will be the same as the sign for q. If we want to find the potential difference ΔV between any two points near an isolated point charge, all we need to do is apply this equation to each point and then subtract one potential from the other.

Potential due to a group of point charges:

Using the principle of superposition, we can find the net potential due to a group of point charges at any given point. All we need to do is take the equation for a single point charge, $V = \frac{1}{4\pi\epsilon_0}\frac{q}{r}$, and then add up these. So, our equation for potential due to a group of point charges is: $V = \sum_{i=1}^{n} V_i = \frac{1}{4\pi\epsilon_0}\sum_{i=1}^{n}\frac{q_i}{r_i}$. The sum of this equation is an algebraic sum, rather than the vector sum that we would use to calculate the electric field resulting from a group of point charges. This is one of the advantages that potential has over electric field: it is much easier to add up several scalar quantities than to add vector quantities where direction must be taken into account.

Potential due to electric dipole:

We can apply the equation for potential due to a group of point charges to find the potential of a point P outside an electric dipole. For the most part, we will only be concerned with situations in which the point is very far from the dipole; that is, situations in which $r \gg d$. When this is the case, we can approximate that: $V = \frac{1}{4\pi\epsilon_0}\frac{p\cos\theta}{r^2}$, in which p is the magnitude of the electric dipole moment. Vector p will be along the dipole axis, pointing from the negative to the positive charge. Because of the nature of symmetry, potential at P will not vary even if P is rotated around the z axis, as long as r and θ are constant. This is because a test charge lying in this plane will always be equidistant from the positive and negative charges of the dipole.

Potential due to continuous charge distribution:

If the charge distribution through an object is continuous, then we cannot use the equation for potential due to a group of point charges. Instead, if we are trying to find the potential V at some point P, we will have to select a differential element of charge dq, and then determine the potential dV at P due to dq, and then integrate over the entire continuous charge distribution. If we say that the zero of potential is at infinity, then, and we treat dq as if it were a point charge, then we can find potential dV: $dV = \dfrac{1}{4\pi \in_0} \dfrac{dq}{r}$. In order to find the potential V at P, then, we integrate to sum the potentials over the total charge distribution:

$V = \int dV = \dfrac{1}{4\pi \in_0} \int \dfrac{dq}{r}$.

Calculating electric field from potential:

If we know the electric potential of a region, we should be able to calculate the electric field for that region. To show how, let us imagine a positive test charge q_0 moving through displacement ds, from one equipotential surface to the adjacent equipotential surface. During this move, the work done on the test charge by the electric field will be $-q_0 dV$, which we can incorporate into the equation: $E \cos \theta = \dfrac{-dV}{ds}$. Since we know that $E \cos \theta$ is the component of E along the s axis that extends through ds, we can create the equation:

$E_s = -\dfrac{\partial V}{\partial s}$. In words, this states that the component of E in any direction is the negative of the rate of change of the electric potential with distance in that direction.

Electric potential energy due to a system of point charges:

Now, let us attempt to find the electric potential energy of a system of charges due to the electric field produced by those charges themselves. For example, if we were to push together two bodies with the same electric charge, then the work we performed would be stored as electric potential energy in the two-charge system. The electric potential energy of a system of fixed point charges is equal to the work that must be done by some external agent to assemble the system, bringing each charge in from an infinite distance. The

equation used to represent this relation is: $$U = W = \frac{1}{4\pi\epsilon_0}\frac{q_1 q_2}{r}.$$

Van de Graaf accelerator

The Van de Graaf accelerator is a machine used for generating potential differences of several million volts. When charged particles are allowed to fall through this potential difference, a beam of energetic particles is produced. These beams have a number of uses: in medicine, they are used to treat certain kinds of cancer, while in physics laboratories they are often used to smash atoms. A Van de Graaf accelerator is set up by placing a small conducting shell with radius r inside a larger conducting shell with radius R. These two shells will have charges q and Q, respectively. If a conducting path is placed between the two shells, all of q will pass to the outer shell. This can be repeated over and over again, increasing the potential of the shells every time.

Capacitors

When we think of potential energy being stored, we probably visualize a spring being compressed or an object being lifted off of the ground. However, potential energy can also be stored in an electric field, with the aid of a capacitor. One classic example of a capacitor is in a photographic flash. Here the capacitor slowly accumulates charge, increasing the electric field until it is time to release it in the form of the flash. There are scores of other uses for capacitors in electronics, however. The tuning mechanisms of radios and TVs and the memory banks of computers both make use of capacitors. A basic capacitor contains two isolated conductors, called plates. When these plates are charged, they will have equal but opposite charges.

Charging a capacitor:

The two plates of a capacitor are equipotential surfaces, and there will be a potential difference between them. For historical reasons, this potential difference is expressed V, rather than ΔV. Charge and potential difference are proportional to one another: $q = CV$, where C is the proportionality constant known as capacitance. The capacitance of a particular capacitor will depend on the geometry of the plates. Capacitance is measured in SI units coulomb per volt, or farad. A capacitor is typically charged by placing it in an electric circuit with a battery. In such a circuit, the potential difference between the plates of the capacitor will be the same as the difference between the two terminals of the battery. At this point, the current ceases and the capacitor is said to be fully charged.

Calculating capacitance

Electric field:

We are now attempting to calculate the capacitance of a capacitor once we know its geometry. In order to do this more easily, we may make a couple of assumptions in calculating the electric field. First, we know that the electric field E between the plates will be related to the charge q on the plates by Gauss' law: $\epsilon_0 \oint E \cdot dA = q$. In all the capacitor-related cases that we will consider, however, the Gaussian surface will be such that whenever electric flux passes through it, the vectors E and dA will be parallel, meaning that the equation can be reduced to: $q = \epsilon_0 EA$, where A is the part of the Gaussian surface through which the flux passes.

Potential difference:

In order to simplify our calculations of capacitance, we can make a few assumptions about potential difference. For one thing, we know that the potential difference between the plates is related to electric field E by: $V_f - V_i = -\int_i^f E \cdot ds$. Since we know in this case that

$V_f - V_i$ will be negative, then we can set this part of the equation up $-V$, and our total

equation can be reset: $V = \int_+^- Eds$. In this equation, the plus and minus signs remind us that

the path of integration starts on the positive plate and ends on the negative plate.

Parallel-plate capacitor:

Let us imagine a capacitor with plates so large and close together that E can be assumed to

be constant throughout the space between the two plates. If we imagine a Gaussian surface

enclosing the charge q on the positive plate, then we may say that $q = \epsilon_0 EA$, and therefore

potential difference may be calculated: $V = \int_+^- Eds = E\int_0^d ds = Ed$. Substituting q from the first

equation and V from the second equation, we can take the basic equation for capacitance

$q = CV$ and convert it into: $C = \epsilon_0 \dfrac{A}{d}$. This is the equation for a parallel-plate capacitor.

Cylindrical capacitor:

Let us imagine a capacitor created by two coaxial cylinders with radii a and b, and with

length L. Each plate will hold an equal but opposite charge q. For our Gaussian surface, we

choose a cylinder with length L and radius r, such that $a \prec r \prec b$. Our equation for electric

field can then be: $q = \epsilon_0 EA$, in which $2\pi rL$ is the area of the curved part of the Gaussian

surface. If we solve this for E, we get: $E = \dfrac{q}{2\pi \epsilon_0 Lr}$. Then, by substituting this result into the

equation for calculating potential difference in a capacitor, we will arrive at

$C = 2\pi \epsilon_0 \dfrac{L}{\ln(b/a)}$, our equation for calculating the capacitance of a cylindrical capacitor.

Spherical capacitor:

Let us imagine a capacitor composed of two concentric spherical shells. Our Gaussian

surface will be another concentric sphere with a radius in between the radii of the two shells. If we calculate for charge using the special equation for capacitors, we get:

$q = \epsilon_0\, EA = \epsilon_0\, E(4\pi r^2)$. This equation can be solved for E: $E = \dfrac{1}{4\pi \epsilon_0} \dfrac{q}{r^2}$. If we combine this

equation with the special equation for finding potential difference in a capacitor, and then

rearrange to solve for capacitance, we will end up with: $C = 4\pi \epsilon_0 \dfrac{ab}{b-a}$, the equation for

calculating capacitance in a spherical capacitor.

Isolated sphere:

We may consider a single isolated spherical conductor of radius R as a capacitor if we

imagine that its corresponding plate is a conducting sphere with infinite radius. This

makes some sense, since we know that the field lines leaving the surface of a charged

isolated conductor will have to end somewhere. In order to find the capacitance of this

conductor, we will first rewrite the equation for a spherical capacitor as: $C = 4\pi \epsilon_0 \dfrac{ab}{b-a}$.

Assuming, then, that b stretches out to infinity, and substituting R for a, we find: $C = 4\pi \epsilon_0\, R$.

Capacitors in parallel:

Sometimes, a group of capacitors that are being used in a circuit can be replaced with a

single equivalent capacitor. One example of this occurs when capacitors are connected in

parallel. Connected capacitors are said to be in parallel when a potential difference that is

applied across their combination results in that potential difference being applied across

each capacitor. If we are trying to find the single capacitance that is equivalent to a parallel

combination, then we can use the equation: $C_{eq} = \displaystyle\sum_{j=1}^{n} C_j$, in which n is the number of

capacitors in parallel. This measure is found by adding up all of the individual capacitances

of the various capacitors in parallel.

Capacitors in series:

Sometimes, we may want to find an equivalent capacitor for a group of capacitors that are

in series. Capacitors are said to be in series when a potential difference that is applied

across the combination is the sum of the resulting potential differences across each

- 87 -

capacitor. Calculating the equivalent capacitance is quite simple: we simply calculate

capacitance for each capacitor $V_1 = \dfrac{q}{C_1}, V_2 = \dfrac{q}{C_2}, \ldots$, then calculate potential difference

$V = V_1 + V_2 + \cdots$, which, when rearranged according to the equation for capacitance, gives us:

$C_{eq} = \dfrac{q}{v} = \dfrac{1}{1/C_1 + 1/C_2 + \cdots}$. This equation can be extended for n number of capacitors:

$\dfrac{1}{C_{eq}} = \displaystyle\sum_{j=1}^{n} \dfrac{1}{C_j}$. Equivalent series capacitance will always be less than the lease capacitance in

the series of capacitors.

Storing energy in an electric field

Obviously, work must be performed by some external agent to charge a capacitor. We can

visualize this work as being stored in the form of electric potential energy U in the electric

field between the two plates. This energy can be recovered at any time, simply by

discharging the capacitor in the circuit. If we imagine, for instance, that charge q' has been

transferred from one plate to the other, then we know that potential difference V' between

the two plates at that particular instant will be q'/C. If an extra increment of charge is

added, the increment of work require will be: $dW = V'dq' = \dfrac{q}{C} dq'$. Work is stored as potential

energy U in the capacitor, such that $U = \dfrac{q^2}{2C}$. This equation can also be written: $U = \dfrac{1}{2}CV^2$.

Energy density

In a parallel-plate capacitor, we may assume that the electric field between the plates will

have a uniform energy density or potential energy per unit volume. Energy density is

expressed u, and can be found by dividing the total potential energy by volume Ad of the

space between the plates. This gives us: $u = \dfrac{U}{Ad} = \dfrac{CV^2}{2Ad}$. If we combine this with $C = \epsilon_0 \dfrac{A}{d}$, we find that it can be written: $u = \frac{1}{2}\epsilon_0 \left(\frac{V}{d}\right)^2$. However, V/d is the electric field, so we may

actually write our equation for energy density: $u = \frac{1}{2}\epsilon_0 E^2$.

Dielectric

A dielectric is an insulating material. If a dielectric substance, like plastic or mineral oil, is placed in between the plates of a capacitor, then, oddly, the capacitance will increase by κ, the dielectric constant of the material. A dielectric introduced between two plates of a capacitor will also place a ceiling on the amount of potential difference that can be applied between the plates. If this value is exceeded, then the dielectric material will break down and form a conducting path. Michael Faraday determined that when a dielectric completely fills the space between the two plates, $C = \kappa\epsilon_0 L = \kappa C_{air}$, where L is the length and C_{air} is the value of capacitance when there is air between the plates.

Atomic view of dielectrics:

When a dielectric is placed into an electric field, one of two things will happen. One possibility is that the electric dipoles within the dielectric will tend to line up with the external electric field. This happens in what are called polar dielectrics. In such substances, alignment will increase as either the strength of the applied field is increased or the temperature is decreased. If the dielectric is what is called a nonpolar dielectric, then small dipole will be created inside the dielectric, but the overall effect will be to weaken the applied field. Even though dipoles are being created within a nonpolar dielectric, the dielectric as whole will remain electrically neutral and there will be no excess charge.

Electric current

An electric current is simply an electric charge in motion. Electric current cannot exist unless there is a difference in electric potential. If, for instance, we have an isolated conducting loop, it will all be at the same potential. No electric field will be able to exist within it or parallel to its surface, and there will be no current. If, however, we should insert a battery into this loop, then the conducting loop will no longer be at a single electric potential. Electric fields will act inside the material that makes up the loop, exerting force on the conducting electrons and establishing a current. This flow of electrons will very quickly reach a steady state. At that point, it will be completely analogous to steady-state fluid flow.

Equation for electric current:

Let us imagine a small section of a conducting loop, in which a current has been established. If the charge dq passes through the hypothetical plane aa' in time dt, then the current through that hypothetical plane can be defined: $i = \dfrac{dq}{dt}$. Under steady-state conditions, current will be the same for any plane that passes through the conductor completely, regardless of location or orientation. This falls out of the idea that charge is always conserved. In other words, for every electron that enters the conductor, one must fall out the other end. The SI unit for current is the coulomb per second, or ampere (A). Current is a scalar quantity, since both charge and time are scalars. This is so even when arrows are used to describe which way a certain current is flowing.

Directions of currents:

When we are depicting the direction that an electric current flows, we must be mindful of the fact that positive and negative charge carriers move in opposite directions. The general rule in notation is that the current arrow is drawn in the direction in which positive carriers would move, even if the actual carriers are not positive. This rule is made possible by the fact that a positive charge carrier moving from right to left will always have the same external effect as a negative carrier moving from left to right. Positive charge carriers will be repelled by the positive terminal of a battery and will be attracted by the negative terminal. The exact opposite holds true for negative charge carriers.

Current density:

Sometimes, rather than analyzing the current i in a particular conductor, we will be more interested in the flow of charge within a particular point of that conductor. A positive charge carrier at some given point will flow in the direction of the electric field E at that point. In order to accurately describe this flow, we have to introduce the concept of current density (J), a vector quantity pointing in the direction of the electric field. If, in a simple case, current is uniformly distributed over a cross-section of uniform conductor, then current density is constant for all points: $J = i/A$, where A is the cross-sectional area of the conductor. The SI unit for current density is the ampere per square meter. For any surface, regardless of whether it is planar, current density is related to current: $i = \int J \cdot dA$, where the area vector dA is assumed to be perpendicular to the surface element of differential area dA.

Calculating drift speed:

The directed flow, or drift speed, of current is generally much smaller than the velocities of the individual electrons in the current. One simple example is of drift speed a uniform wire through which a charge is moving. We will imagine that the positive charge carriers are moving with constant drift speed v_d. The number of carriers in a length L of wire will be nAL, where n is the number of carriers per unit volume and A is the cross-sectional area of the wire. We may therefore say that a charge of magnitude $\Delta q = (nAL)e$ passes through this volume in the time interval given by $\Delta t = L/v_d$. We may then say that the current in the wire is $i = \dfrac{\Delta q}{\Delta t} = \dfrac{nALe}{L/v_d} = nAev_d$. If we solve for drift speed, we can arrive at: $J = (ne)v_d$, in which the product ne is the carrier charge density. This is measured in the SI units coulombs per cubic meter.

Resistance

If we were to apply the exact same potential difference between the ends of two geometrically similar rods, one made of copper and one made of glass, we would create vastly different currents. This is because these two substances have different resistances. The resistance of a conductor may be determined between any two points by applying a potential difference V between those points and measuring the resulting current. Resistance, then, can be calculated: $R = V / i$. The SI unit for resistance is the volt per ampere, or ohm (Ω). When a conductor is placed into a circuit to provide a specific resistance, it is known as a resistor. For a given potential difference, the greater the resistance is to the current, the smaller will be the current.

Resistivity:

Sometimes when we are studying the function of a resistor, we will not want to find the current through the resistor, but rather on the electric field created at that point. In other words, we will want to ignore potential difference in favor of looking at the current density at that particular point. If this is the case, we are studying the resistivity (ρ) of the substance. Resistivity is calculated: $\rho = E / J$. The SI unit for resistivity is the ohm-meter, or $\Omega \, m$. The above equation can also be written in vector form: $E = \rho J$. When we refer to the conductivity of a substance, we are simply referring to the reciprocal of its resistivity. Conductivity is measured: $\sigma = 1 / \rho$, and is measured in reciprocal ohm-meters.

Calculating resistance:

If we know the resistivity of a particular substance, we should be able to calculate the resistance of a length of wire of a given diameter made of that substance. For instance, if we have a cross-sectional area A of wire, with length L and potential difference V between its two ends, the electric field and current density will be constant throughout the wire and will have the values: $E = V / L$ and $J = i / A$. We can then factor in resistivity ρ and arrive at an equation for the resistance of the wire: $R = \rho \dfrac{L}{A}$. It should be noted that this equation can

- 92 -

only be used when we are dealing with a homogenous wire of uniform cross-sectional area.

Variations with temperature:

The resistivity of a particular substance will vary depending on temperature. For most metals, the relation between resistivity and temperature is linear over a fairly broad range. In most cases, then, we can get by with this equation: $\rho - \rho_0 = \rho_0 \alpha (T - T_0)$, where T_0 is a selected reference temperature and ρ_0 is the resistivity at that temperature. Since temperature is used only as a difference in this equation, it does not matter whether the Celsius or Kelvin scale is used. The quantity α in this equation is known as the temperature coefficient of resistivity. There are various values for this coefficient for different metals.

Resistances in series:

Sometimes, a circuit may contain more than one resistor, set up in a series. Connected resistances are said to be in a series when a potential difference applied across the combination is the sum of the resulting potential differences across the individual resistances. When this is the case, we may need to seek out an equivalent resistance to these multiple resistors. This means we are looking for a single resistor that won't diminish the amount of current in the circuit any more or less than the existing resistors.

The equation for equivalent resistance is: $R_{eq} = \sum_{j=1}^{n} R_j$, where n is the number of resistances in the series. We can note that resistances in series will follow the same rules as capacitors in parallel.

Ohm's law

A resistor is a conductor that provides a specific resistance regardless of the magnitude and direction (polarity) of the applied potential difference. Some conductors, however, will vary in resistance depending on the applied potential difference. If we study such devices, we will gain a few insights, insights which have been systematized as Ohm's law. First,

Ohm's law states that the current flowing through a device is directly proportional to the potential difference applied to the device. We can then say that a conducting device obeys Ohm's law when its resistance is independent of the magnitude an polarity of the applied potential difference. The conducting material, on the other hand, can be said to obey Ohm's law when its resistivity is independent of the magnitude and direction of the applied electric field.

Electric circuits

As a current moves around a circuit from one battery terminal to the other, the electric potential energy will decrease in magnitude by the amount $dU = dqV = idtV$. According to the principle of conservation of energy, the decrease in electric potential must be accompanied by a transfer of energy to some other form. In this case, the power associated with that transfer can be calculated: $P = iV$. This power is transferred to some unspecified device: a motor or a storage battery, perhaps. Sometimes, the circuit will lose some potential energy as thermal energy; in this case, energy is dissipated and cannot be brought back. In such cases, we can calculate the dissipation of the energy with either $P = i^2R$ or

$$P = \frac{V^2}{R}.$$

Emf devices

In order to maintain a constant flow of charge carriers through a resistor, we must create a potential difference between the two ends. A device that maintains this difference by doing work on the charge carriers is known as an emf device. Emf devices (also known as seats of emf), derive their name from the phrase electromotive force. A battery is a very common example of an emf device, as is an electric generator or a solar cell. Interestingly, emf devices are not limited to technology or to the man-made world: all kinds of animals, from human beings to electric eels, have physiological emf devices inside of them. Emf devices may vary widely in their methods of operation, but they nonetheless all perform the same basic function: to maintain a potential difference between their terminals.

Ideal and real:

- An ideal emf device is one that does not have any internal resistance to the internal movement of charge from one terminal to the other. In such cases, the potential difference between the terminals is equal to the emf of the device. The emf of the emf device is defined: $\xi = \dfrac{dW}{dq}$.

- A real emf device, on the other hand, is one in which there is an internal resistance to the internal movement of charge. A battery is a good example of a real emf device. When a real emf device is not part of a circuit, and does not have any current running through it, then the potential difference between its terminals will be different than its emf.

The SI unit of emf is the joule per coulomb, or volt.

Calculating current

Energy method:

Let us imagine a simple circuit composed of an ideal battery B with emf ξ, a resistor of resistance R, and two connecting wires. One way to calculate the current in this circuit is to consider the rules of energy conservation. We can use the equation $P = i^2 R$ to show that in time interval dt an amount of energy $i^2 R$ will move appear in the resistor as thermal energy. During the same time interval, the charge $dq = idt$ will move through the battery, and the battery will have done work on the charge equal to $dW = \xi dq = \xi idt$. The work done by the battery must equal the thermal energy that appears in the resistor, meaning $\xi = iR$, meaning emf is the energy per unit charge that is transferred to the moving charges by the battery. The quantity iR is the energy per unit charge transferred from the moving charges to thermal energy within the resistor. . If we solve for I: $i = \dfrac{\xi}{R}$.

- 95 -

Potential method:

Let us imagine a simple circuit composed of an ideal battery B with emf ξ, a resistor of resistance R, and two connecting wires. One way to calculate the current of this circuit is to focus on the concept of potential. If we move all the way around the circuit in either direction, adding the potential differences algebraically as we go, we will end up with zero. This is known as the loop rule. If this is the case, then the potential when we started our loop must be equal to our potential at the end; in other words, the equation $V_a + \xi - iR = V_a$ can be simplified to $\xi - iR = 0$. This gives us two insights: if we mentally pass through a resistance in the direction of the current, change in potential will be –iR; if we move in the opposite direction, change will be +iR. Also, if we move along a circuit in the same direction as the emf arrow, we will have a change in potential equal to $+\xi$; in the opposite direction, change in potential $-\xi$.

Internal resistance

All real emf devices will have some internal resistance. Let us imagine a battery with internal resistance r, wired to an external resistor with resistance R. Since the internal resistance of the battery is a natural feature of the substances of which the battery is made, it cannot be removed. If we apply the loop rule to this circuit, we will arrive at the measure: $\xi - ir - iR = 0$. If we solve this equation for current, we get: $i = \dfrac{\xi}{R+r}$. This equation will reduce to $i = \dfrac{\xi}{R}$ if internal resistance is set to zero. Many physics problems will ignore internal resistance in the interest of simplicity, but it is an inevitable feature of real batteries.

Potential differences:

Often, we will need to find the potential difference between two different points in a circuit. For instance, if we wanted to move from point a to point b in a circuit, passing through resistor R, we could calculate the potential difference: $V_b - V_a = +iR$. Combining this with the

- 96 -

equation for current with internal resistance, we get: $V_b - V_a = \xi \dfrac{R}{R+r}$. In order to find the potential difference between any two points in a circuit, then, we can start at one point and traverse the circuit to the other, following any path, and then add algebraically the changes in potential that we encounter.

Measuring instruments for circuits

There a few different instruments that are commonly used to measure current in a circuit.

- An ammeter is a device that measures current by having the current pass through it; sometimes you have to cut the wire in order to use an ammeter. The resistance of the ammeter must be very small compared to the resistances of the other objects in the circuit.

- A voltmeter is used to measure potential difference. In order to find potential difference between any two points in a circuit, one simply has to connect the two terminals of the voltmeter at those two spots without breaking the circuit.

- Finally, a potentiometer is used to measure emf. It does so by comparing the emf of a given device with a known standard. It does so by briefly replacing the normal emf device and assessing the change in current.

RC circuits

Charging a capacitor:

Some currents are made so that they will vary according to time. If we are to charge a capacitor for such a circuit, we must take careful steps. First, we must put a capacitor with capacitance C in the circuit, such that when a switch is thrown a battery is put into series circuit with the capacitor and resistor. The equation that we can use to describe the

charging is: $R\dfrac{dq}{dt} + \dfrac{q}{C} = \xi$. This equation describes the variation with time of charge q on the capacitor. The solution of this equation is $q = C\xi(1-e^{-t/RC})$. The derivative of q(t) is:

$$i = \frac{dq}{dt} = \left(\frac{\xi}{R}\right)e^{-t/RC}$$

.

Time constant:

In the equations for charging a capacitor, RC is known as the capacitive time constant of the circuit, and it is represented with the symbol τ. This is the time at which the charge on the capacitor has increased to a factor of $(1-e^{-1})$, about 63% of its fully charged value. If we substitute this into the equation for charging a capacitor, we arrive at: $q = C\xi(1-e^{-1}) = 0.63C\xi$. And, because $C\xi$ is equal to the equilibrium charge on the capacitor, which corresponds to $t \rightarrow \infty$ in that equation for charging a capacitor, we can say that the value for RC has been proved.

Charging process:

Let us take a more common sense look at the charging process in an RC circuit. When the switch is first closed, there will be no charge in the capacitor and therefore no potential difference between its plates. For this reason, the loop rule will show that potential difference across the resistor is equal to the emf of the battery, and the current through the resistor is ξ/R. After the onset of current, however, charges will begin to appear on the capacitor plates and a potential difference q/C will develop between them. During this process, the potential across the resistor will decrease, and so the current through it will stop. These changes will continue until the capacitor is fully charged. At this point, the potential across the capacitor will be the same as the emf of the battery, and there will be no current in the circuit.

Discharging a capacitor:

If we assume that the capacitor in an RC circuit has been fully charged, such that it is equal to the potential difference of the battery, then we must develop some equations to describe the discharging of the energy from the capacitor through the resistor. The equations we used for charging will still hold up, although there will no longer be an emf device in the circuit. Adjusting the equation for this reason, we find: $R\dfrac{dq}{dt}+\dfrac{q}{C}=0$. The solution to this equation is: $q=q_0e^{-t/RC}$, in which q_0 is the initial charge on the capacitor. Capacitive time constant RC will govern the discharging process as well as the charging process. Current during discharged can be calculated by differentiating the second equation:

$$i=\frac{dq}{dt}=-\frac{q_0}{RC}e^{-t/RC}=-i_0e^{-t/RC}$$
.

Magnetic field

Just as an object that holds an electric charge will produce a vector field, so does a charged magnet. Magnetic field is typically represented with the letter B. One common type of magnet is the electromagnet, in which a coil of wire is wound around an iron core, and electric current is sent through the coil. Permanent magnets are those that do not need a current to exert a magnetic force. Physicists have spent a great deal of time trying to determine where magnetic charges come from, and have found that they come from moving electric charges. So, a magnetic field is set up by an electric current, and if we are to place another moving charge or a wire carrying current into a magnetic field, a magnetic force will act on it.

B (magnetic field):
We will define B, the magnetic field, by measuring the magnetic force exerted on a moving electric charge in that field. This is generally done by firing a test charge into the area where B is to be defined. After a time, we will find that force F_B acting on a test charge of velocity v and charge q can be written: $F_B=qv\times B$, in which q can be either positive or negative. From this equation, we will discover that the magnetic force always acts perpendicular to the velocity vector. This means a magnetic field can neither speed up nor slow down a charged particle; it can only deflect it. Also, a magnetic field will exert no force

on a charge that moves parallel to the field. We can see from this equation that the magnitude of the deflecting force will be: $F_B = qvB\sin\phi$.

Definition of magnetic field:

The equation for defining a magnetic field, $F_B = qv \times B$, provides us with a few special insights. First, we now know that magnetic force always acts perpendicular to the velocity vector. Second, we know that a magnetic field will exert no force on a charge that moves either parallel or antiparallel to the field. Third, we find that the maximum value of the deflecting force will occur when the test charge is moving perpendicular to the magnetic field. Fourth, we find that the magnitude of the deflecting force is directly proportional to q and to v. The greater the charge of the particle, and the greater its speed, the greater will be the magnetic deflecting force. Finally, we will find that the direction of the magnetic deflecting force will depend on the sign of q; that is, positive and negative test charges will be deflected in opposite directions.

Magnetic field lines:

Just as electric fields can be represented with field lines, so may we represent magnetic fields. The same rules will apply, namely that the direction of the tangent to a magnetic field line at any point will give the direction of B at that point; and the spacing of the lines will be proportional to the magnitude of B. In the magnetic field lines drawn on a simple bar magnet, we will find that the lines emerge out of one end, the north pole, and will enter back in through the other end, known as the south pole. These opposite poles of a magnet will attract each other. Considering this, and considering that the north pole of a compass needle (a small bar magnet) will point north, we will see that the Earth's geomagnetic pole in the northern hemisphere is actually a south magnetic pole.

Electrons deflected by a magnetic field:

When an image is displayed on a television screen, this is the result of a beam of electrons being deflected by a magnetic field. When we study the effects of a magnetic field on electrons, we will find that regardless of the sign of the particle, the electric field and the magnetic field will deflect it in opposite directions. The most typical way of measuring this deflection in the laboratory is to propel a beam of electrons by means of a potential difference through a slit in a screen, at which point they will enter a region in which there are electric and magnetic fields set perpendicular to one another. The electron will make a point of light on a screen, whose distance from the spot opposite the screen will give a measure of deflection.

Equations:

If we were to measure the deflection of an electron in a purely electric field, we would find that the level of deflection can be measured $y = \dfrac{qEL^2}{2mv^2}$, in which v is the speed of the electron and L is the length of the plates that are creating the deflection. The direction of the deflection will allow us to determine the sign of the charge of the particle. If the two fields are set to cancel one another out, then we will have $qE = qvB$, which gives us $v = \dfrac{E}{B}$. In this way, the crossed fields allow us to measure the speed of the particles that pass through them. If we eliminate v between the two equations, we will get $\dfrac{m}{q} = \dfrac{B^2 L^2}{2yE}$.

Circulating charge:

Sometimes, electrons will be projected into a chamber, and the magnetic force will continually deflect them in such a way that they follow a circular path. If we apply Newton's second law as it regards circular motion to this scenario, we will get the equation: $qvB = m\dfrac{v^2}{r}$. If we solve for r, we can find the radius of this circular path: $r = \dfrac{mv}{qB}$. Period can be found: $T = \dfrac{2\pi r}{v} = \dfrac{2\pi}{v}\dfrac{mv}{qB} = \dfrac{2\pi m}{qB}$. Frequency can be found: $f = \dfrac{1}{T} = \dfrac{qB}{2\pi m}$. The angular frequency of the motion is: $\omega = 2\pi f = \dfrac{qB}{m}$.

Cyclotron:

In their ongoing quest to determine the basic components of matter, physicists have discovered that one good way to analyze the structure of tiny particles is to either slam them into a solid target, or to slam them into each other. In order to accomplish this, the particles need to be brought to a great speed by causing them to circulate in a magnetic field. A cyclotron is one machine that accomplishes this task. It is composed of two large, D-shaped objects, between which a potential difference is created. These dees, as they are known, are placed in a magnetic field. A charged particle is then place into one of the curved oscillators, such that it is propelled out; at the moment it leaves, however, the dees change their charge, so the charged particle is the propelled back into the original dee. So, a cyclotron will only work effectively when the frequency with which the particle moves back and forth is equal to the frequency of the electric oscillator.

Current-carrying wire:

A magnetic field will exert a sideways force on the conduction electrons in a wire. Since the conduction electrons cannot escape sideways out of the wire, we know that this force must be transmitted bodily to the wire itself. For instance, if we have a wire carrying charge i, and we know that the longitudinal axis of the wire is perpendicular to a magnetic field B, then we know that a force equal to $(-e)v_d B$ will act on each conduction electron. If we were to reverse either the magnetic field or the direction of the current, then the force on the wire would reverse as well. If the magnetic field is not perpendicular to the wire, then we can find the magnetic force with this equation: $F_B = iL \times B$.

Torque on a current loop:

Let us imagine a simple motor, consisting of a single current-carrying loop immersed in magnetic field B. The two magnetic forces F and –F combine to exert a torque on this loop, causing it to rotate about its central axis. If we imagine the loop as a square, then two of the sides will be perpendicular to B, and two of the sides will be parallel. The net force will be the sum of the forces acting on each of the four sides of the loop. On one side, vector L will pointing in the direction of the current and so vector L will have magnitude b. The angle between L and B for this side will be $90^{\circ} - \theta$, and so the magnitude of force acting on this side is: $F = ibB\sin(90^{\circ} - \theta) = ibB\cos\theta$. The force on the side opposite to this will have the same magnitude but the opposite direction, so these will create net force zero.

We have demonstrated that, on the side of a square current loop on which vector L is pointing in the direction of the current, force exerted by magnetic field will be cancelled out by the equal but opposite force on the section of wire that runs parallel. On the other two sections of wire, the situation will be slightly different. Here, the magnitude of force will be iaB for both, though since these forces move in opposite directions they will tend to turn the coil. The resulting net torque will tend to rotate the coil: $\tau = N\tau' = NiabB\sin\theta = (NiA)B\sin\theta$, where $A(=ab)$ is the area enclosed by the loop and N is the number of turns. The quantities in parentheses are grouped together because they are all properties of the coil.

Magnetic dipole:

A current loop upon which a magnetic field is operating can be called a magnetic dipole. In such a case, we would refer to the magnetic dipole moment as having the direction of the normal vector n to the plane of the loop. The magnetic dipole moment is expressed μ, and its magnitude can be found with the equation: $\mu = NiA$. When an external magnetic field is exerting torque on a magnetic dipole, work must be done in order to change the current of the dipole. In other words, the magnetic dipole must have a magnetic potential energy, which will depend on the dipole's orientation in the field. This measure can be found: $U(\theta) = -\mu \cdot B$. Some other common magnetic dipoles include simple bar magnets, electrons, and even the Earth itself.

Calculating magnetic field:

Let us now attempt to calculate the magnetic field that a given distribution of currents will produce in the surrounding space. This is not unlike the task of determining the electric field created by a given distribution of charges. In order to determine the magnetic field B at a point P near a wire carrying current, we will have to break the wire down into differential current elements, corresponding to differential charge elements. The

magnitude of the magnetic field at P will be: $dB = \frac{\mu_0}{4\pi}\frac{ids\sin\theta}{r^2}$, in which μ_0 is the permeability

constant, with the value: $\mu_0 = 4\pi\times10^{-7}T\cdot m/A \approx 1.26\times10^{-6}T\cdot m/A$. The magnitude equation can

be written in vector form: $dB = \left(\frac{\mu_0}{4\pi}\right)\frac{ids\times r}{r^3}$. This is known as the law of Biot and Savart, and

is the typical tool for calculating magnetic field set up at a point by a given distribution of

current.

Magnetic field due to a long straight wire:

The law of Biot and Savart can be used to show that the magnitude of a magnetic field at a

perpendicular distance r from a long straight wire with current i is $B = \frac{\mu_0 i}{2\pi r}$. In this

equation, the magnitude of B depends only on the current and on the perpendicular

distance r from the wire. There is a simple "right-hand" rule for finding the direction of the

magnetic field set up by a current element, such as an element of a long wire: Simply grasp

the element in your right hand with your thumb extended in the direction of the current

(you will be imagining this action, of course). The direction in which your fingers are

curling is the direction of the magnetic field lines due to that element.

Magnetic force on a current-carrying wire:

We know already that a section of long straight wire of length L, with current i, will, if

placed in a uniform magnetic field, experience a deflecting force: $F = iL\times B_{ext}$. The subscript

in this equation is used to make sure that we distinguish the external field from the

intrinsic field set up by the current in the wire itself. If there is no external field, there is no

deflecting action on the wire. We will always be looking for resultant magnetic field B,

which is the vector sum of the external and intrinsic fields: $B = B_{ext} + B_{int}$. Close to the wore,

the intrinsic field will predominate, while farther away the external field will have more

influence.

Two parallel conductors:

Let us determine the magnetic field created by two long parallel wires. Let us say that these wires are separated by a distance d and carry the currents i_a and i_b. The magnitude of the field produced by one wire at the site of the other wire will be: $B_a = \dfrac{\mu_0 i_a}{2\pi d}$. The other wire, then, will experience a magnetic force that can be measured: $F_{ba} = i_b L B_a \cos 0^o$. We could likewise compute the force on the other wire as well as the other magnetic field created. For parallel currents, the forces will be attractive to one another; for anti-parallel forces, the effect will be repulsive.

Energy stored in a magnetic field:

When two long parallel wires carry current in the same direction and attract one another, and we must do work in order to pull them apart, we are storing energy in the magnetic fields of these currents. This energy can be brought back at any time by allowing the wires to return to their original positions. The equation for this energy is $U_B = \dfrac{1}{2} L i^2$, the total energy stored by inductor L carrying current i. We must assume that all of the energy that is not converted into thermal energy will be present in the sum of the energy for this magnetic field.

Energy density:

Let us consider briefly the energy per unit volume stored in a specific part of a magnetic field. If we consider length l near the center of a long solenoid with cross-sectional area A, we can say that Al is the volume associated with this length. Since the magnetic field outside such a solenoid is zero, all of the energy must lie within this volume. Furthermore, this stored energy will have to be uniformly distributed throughout the volume of the solenoid, since the magnetic field is uniform inside the solenoid. The equation for energy density can thus be written $u_B = \dfrac{B^2}{2\mu_0}$. This equation gives us the density of stored energy at any point where the magnetic field is B. This is another case in which the solenoid is useful for creating a uniform field that can be easily analyzed.

Ampere

The ampere is one of the seven basic SI units. Its definition falls out of our consideration of the behavior of two parallel charged wires. The ampere is that constant current which, if it is maintained in two straight parallel conductors of infinite length, of negligible cross-section, and placed exactly one meter apart in a vacuum, would produce on each of these conductors a force equal to 2×10^{-7} newtons per meter of length. In the laboratory, when physicists are trying to measure an ampere, they will use multiturn coils of carefully constructed geometries rather than simulate conductors of infinite length. Of course, this definition for the ampere specifies parallel wires, and therefore attractive forces.

Basic equation of Ampere's law:
Just as in electrostatics we can use Gauss' law to calculate the electric field caused by any charge distribution in cases of great symmetry, in our study of magnetism we may use Ampere's law for select cases. Ampere's law is written: $\oint B \cdot ds = \mu_0 i$. This equation can only be applied to closed loops, which are known as Amperian loops (the circle around the integral sign in the equation indicates that the quantity on that side of the equation is to be integrated around that closed loop). The current i in this equation is the net current encircled by the loop. In a general sense, we will find that Ampere's law relates the distribution of the magnetic field at points on the loop to the current that passes through the loop.

In order to better understand Ampere's law, let us apply it to a specific figure. We will imagine an arbitrary Amperian loop, encircling two wires but excluding a third. We will then divide this loop into differential line segments with length ds. At one of these line elements, the magnetic field will have a particular value, and will lie in the plane of the Amperian loop (that is, perpendicular to the wire). The integral on the left side of Ampere's law will thus become $\oint B \cdot ds = \oint B \cos \theta \, ds$; in other words, we will travel around the loop adding up $B \cos \theta \, ds$. It does not particularly matter which way we choose to go around the loop.

Finding current in Ampere's law:

In order to successfully apply Ampere's law, we will need to determine the net current encircled by an Amperian loop. This can be done by assigning a plus or minus sign to each current that is found in the loop, and then traveling around the loop adding up these currents. We can use a simple right-hand rule to determine how to assign the signs: curl the fingers of your right hand around the loop in the direction of the integration. Any current passing through the loop in the general direction of your thumb is assigned a plus sign, and any current moving in the opposite direction is given a negative sign. This rule is somewhat arbitrary, but it ensures that physicists always go about tallying current in the same way.

Solenoid:

One common situation in which Ampere's law can be applied usefully involves the tightly-wound coil known as the solenoid. We will assume that the length of a solenoid is much greater than its diameter. The magnetic field created by a solenoid will be the vector sum of the fields set up by the individual turns in the coil. At points very close to the wire, the magnetic field will be almost like that created by a long straight wire, and the lines of B will resemble concentric circles. The field will tend to cancel out between adjacent turns, and at points inside the solenoid and reasonably far from the wire, the field lines may be approximately parallel to the central axis. In the case of an ideal solenoid (one which is infinitely long), the field inside will be uniform and parallel to the solenoid axis. The magnetic field of a solenoid can be found: $B = \mu_0 i_0 n$.

Toroid:

A toroid is simply a solenoid that has been bent into a doughnut shape. Ampere's law, along with some fundamental observations about symmetry, will give us a picture of the magnetic field created by this object. Symmetry suggests to us that B will form concentric circles inside a toroid. If we take one concentric circle as an Amperian loop, Ampere's law will give us $(B)(2\pi r) = \mu_0 i_0 N$, in which i_0 is the current in the toroid windings and N is the total number of turns. This will yield: $B = \dfrac{\mu_0 i_0 N}{2\pi}\dfrac{1}{r}$. Unlike in a solenoid, B will not be constant over the cross-section of a toroid. Instead, we will find that B=0 for points outside of an ideal toroid.

Biot-Savart law:

In the case of a current loop acting as a magnetic dipole, there will not be enough symmetry to allow for the use of Ampere's law, and so we will be forced to rely on the law of Biot and Savart. We will consider only points on the axis of the loop, which we will name the z axis. We can find the magnitude of the magnetic field: $B(z) = \dfrac{\mu_0 i R^2}{2(R^2 + z^2)^{3/2}}$, in which R is the radius of the circular loop and z is the distance of the point in question from the center of the loop. The direction of B will be the same as the direction of the magnetic dipole moment. This equation can be written in vector form: $B(z) = \dfrac{\mu_0}{2\pi}\dfrac{\mu}{z^3}$.

Faraday's law of induction

If we place a closed conducting loop in an external magnetic field and then rotate the loop by exerting a torque on it, an electric current will be created in the loop. The physical law that describes the construction of this current is known as Faraday's law of induction. This provides a nice symmetry with the fact that if we sent a current through a closed conducting loop in an external magnetic field, a torque will be exerted on it. The SI unit of inductance is called the henry (H). Energy can be converted from inductive and capacitive forms with the use of a device called an electromagnetic oscillator. Faraday's law of induction will yield several other insights into the relation between electricity and magnetism.

First experiment:

There are two basic experiments that demonstrate Faraday's law of induction. In the first experiment, a wire loop has its two terminals connected to a device, called a galvanometer, that can detect the presence of current in the loop. Since there is no battery in this circuit, we would expect this meter to read a current. However, if a bar magnet is placed near the loop, the meter will move. The deflection registered by the meter will be proportional to the speed with which the meter is moved. Moreover, if the magnet is reversed, then the meter will read an equal but opposite current. What seems to matter is the relative motion of magnet and loop. The current that is produced in the loop is called induced current, and the work done per unit charge in moving this current through the loop is called induced emf.

Second experiment:

In the first experiment for proving Faraday's law of induction, we attached a galvanometer to the two terminals of a simple wire loop and observed the current produced by the motion relative to a bar magnet. Another experiment proving this law can be conducted by using the same galvanometer-loop system, but placing another loop attached to a battery close by. When a switch is thrown, producing a current in the second loop, the galvanometer will briefly register a current in the first loop. If the current is turned off, the galvanometer will again deflect momentarily. In other words, only a change in current in the second loop is an induced emf for the second loop. These two experiments force us to conclude that emf is only induced when something is changing.

Insights:

Referring back to our two equations proving Faraday's law of induction, we observe that an emf is induced in an uncharged loop only when the number of magnetic field lines passing through that loop is changing. The specific number of field lines that is passing through a loop at any time interval is of no importance; all that matters is that the value is changing. The value of the induced emf will be determined by the rate of change of the magnetic field lines. This assertion is supported by the experiments: in the first experiment, for instance, the galvanometer registered a current when the magnet was moved towards or away from the loop, but returned to zero if the magnet was held stationary at a point close to the loop.

Quantitative treatment:

Let us consider a surface bounded by a closed conducting loop. We can represent the number of magnetic lines passing through that surface with magnetic flux Φ_B, such that $\Phi_B = \int B \cdot dA$, where dA is a differential element of the surface area, and the integration is carried out over the entire surface. If we suppose that the magnetic field has the same magnitude throughout a planar surface of area A, and is perpendicular to that surface, then we can say reduce our equation to: $\Phi_B = BA$. The SI unit for magnetic flux is the tesla meter squared, otherwise known as the weber. Faraday's law can now state that the emf induced in a conducting loop is equal to the negative of the rate at which the magnetic flux through that loop is changing with time. In equation form: $\xi = -\dfrac{d\Phi_B}{dt}$.

Electric potential:

We know that induced electric fields are created by a changing magnetic flux rather than any static charge. Though this kind of field will exert a force on a test charge, there are some differences between it and a field created by static charge. For one thing, the field lines of induced electric fields will produce closed loops, which will never happen with the fields lines produced by static charges. We may also say generally that electric potential has meaning only for electric fields that are produced by static charges; it does not have any meaning for those electric fields that are produced by induction. This is clear if we remember the equation for potential difference: $V_f - V_i = \dfrac{W_{if}}{q_0} = -\int_i^f E \cdot ds$. In the case of a closed loop, however, V_i and V_f will have the same value, which would make the integral zero. This cannot be so.

Lenz's law

Lenz's law will help us to further understand the phenomenon of induction. Specifically, Lenz's law helps us determine the direction of an induced current in a closed conducting loop. It asserts that an induced current in a closed conducting loop will appear in such a direction that it opposes the charge that produced it. This notion of opposition is symbolized by the minus sign in Faraday's law. It is important to note that Lenz's law refers to induced currents rather than induced emfs. This means that it can only be directly applied to closed conducting loops. In situations where the loop is not closed, physicists will generally just find the direction of the induced emf by considering what would happen if the loop were closed.

First experiment for Faraday's law:
In order to more accurately understand Lenz's law, let us apply it to the system outlined in the first experiment for Faraday's law of induction: a galvanometer attached to a simple wire loop. We will note that the push of the magnet is the change that produces the induced current, and the current will act to oppose that push. If the magnet is pulled away from the coil, the induced current will oppose this pull by forming a south pole on the face of the loop opposing the magnet. We will also note that the induced magnetic field does not oppose the magnetic field of the magnet; it merely opposes the change in the magnetic field. If the magnet is withdrawn, then this decrease in magnetic flux will be opposed by the induced magnetic field through a reinforcement of the field.

Energy conservation:
Let us imagine what would happen if Lenz's law were turned around, and the induced current acted to aid the change that produced it. If this were the case, then we would only need to barely push a stationary magnet to set it in motion, and its motion would then be

self-perpetuating. This magnet would accelerate towards the loop in the first experiment for Faraday's law, and it would gain kinetic energy as it went. Of course, this would create a situation in which something was being created from nothing, which never happens in physics. Indeed, Lenz's law can be seen as a statement of the principle of conservation of energy for situations in which there are currents induced through a circuit.

Induction

Rate of doing work:

In order to take a quantitative look at induction, let us imagine a rectangular loop of wire with width L, one end of which is in a uniform external magnetic field directed perpendicularly into the plane of the loop. This loop will then be pulled away from the field with velocity v. If this is to be done at a constant speed, then a constant force must be applied as well, since a force of equal magnitude but opposite direction will act on the loop at the same time. As the loop is moved out of the field, however, the flux through the loop will decrease, and a current will be produced in the loop. This current can be calculated:

$i = \dfrac{BLv}{R}$. Isolating the force opposed to our work, we can measure it as: $F = \dfrac{B^2 L^2 v}{R}$, which we can then use to get the equation for the rate of work done: $P = Fv = \dfrac{B^2 L^2 v^2}{R}$.

Thermal energy:

Returning to the scenario in which we are slowly pulling a wire loop out of a magnetic field, we may want to find the rate at which thermal energy will appear in the loop as it is pulled along at a constant speed. If we take the equation $P = i^2 R$, and then substitute for i, then we find: $P = \left(\dfrac{BLv}{R}\right)^2 R = \dfrac{B^2 L^2 v^2}{R}$, which is precisely the same as the rate at which work is being done on the loop. In other words, the work that is done pulling the loop through the magnetic field will appear as thermal energy in the loop, creating a small rise in temperature.

Induced electric fields:

If we place a copper ring with radius r in a uniform external magnetic field, and increase the strength of the field at a steady rate, then the magnetic flux through the ring will change at a steady rate and an induced current and induced emf will appear in the ring. If there is a current in the copper ring, then we may assume that an electric field is present at various points within the ring, and it must have been produced by the magnetic flux. This induced electric field will be exactly the same as any other electric field. This scenario asserts another useful formulation of Faraday's law, namely that a changing magnetic field produces an electric field. Interestingly, this electric field will be created even if there is no copper ring.

Inductors

A capacitor, we may remember, is an arrangement that we can use to create a certain electric field in a given region of space. In a similar way, an inductor is an arrangement that can be used to produce a magnetic field. We will see that energy can be stored in the magnetic field of an inductor in much the same way that it can be stored in the electric field of a capacitor. For the most part, we will use a long solenoid (or, more accurately, a short section of a very long solenoid) as our example of an inductor. When a capacitor is attached to a battery and a resistor in series, it will not immediately reach its equilibrium state, but will approach it exponentially. This same process will occur if an inductor is connected to a battery and resistor in series.

Inductance:

If a current is established through the turns of an inductor, there will be a magnetic flux Φ due to that current through the windings, and the windings can be said to be linked by this shared flux. The inductance of the inductor can be defined: $L = \dfrac{N\Phi}{i}$, where N is the number of turns. The product $N\Phi$ is called the flux linkage. This similar to what happens when equal and opposite charges are placed on the plates of a capacitor, so that a potential difference appears between the plates (this capacitance is measured $C = \dfrac{q}{V}$. Since the SI unit of magnetic flux is the tesla-meter squared, we can say that the SI unit of inductance is the tesla-meter squared per ampere, otherwise known as the henry.

Solenoid:

We can use the equation for inductance to determine the inductance per unit length of a long solenoid with cross section A. In order to do so, however, we need to establish the number of flux linkages set up by a given current in the solenoid windings. For a given length l, the number of flux linkages will be: $N\Phi = (nl)(BA)$. B can be determined from the equation $B = \mu_0 i n$, and so, using the equation for inductance: $L = \dfrac{N\Phi}{i} = \dfrac{(nl)(BA)}{i} = \dfrac{(nl)(\mu_0 in)(A)}{i}$. Thus, the equation for inductance per unit length for a long solenoid near its center is: $L/l = \mu_0 n^2 A$.

Toroid:

We can modify our equation for inductance to find the inductance of a toroid. First, though, we must calculate the number of flux linkages that are set up by the given current. In order to do so, we must find out how the magnetic field within the toroid depends on the current in its windings. We can determine this by using the equation for a magnetic field in a toroid (where the magnetic field will not be uniform) is given by: $B = \dfrac{\mu_0 iN}{2\pi r}$. We find the flux over the toroid cross section by integration, and inductance can then be defined: $L = \dfrac{\mu_0 N^2 h}{2\pi} \ln \dfrac{b}{a}$. We see here that induction can be written as the permeability constant μ_0 multiplied by a quantity with the dimensions of a length.

Self-induction:

If two coils are set up near one another, then a current in one coil will set up a magnetic flux through the other coil. Also, if the current in that coil is changed, an emf will be

- 114 -

induced in the coil in which the current was changed. This process is known as self-induction, and the emf it produces is called self-induced emf. This emf will obey Faraday's law of induction just like any other induced emf. This quantity can be defined: $\xi_L = -L \frac{di}{dt}$. In short, a self-induced emf will appear any time the current changes in an inductor. The direction of a self-induced emf can be found using Lenz's law; the minus sign in the above equation represents the fact that, as Lenz's law states, the self-induced emf will act to oppose the change that brings it about.

RL circuits:

If we construct a single-loop circuit containing a resistor R and an inductor L, we will find that it behaves in way that is analogous to an RC circuit (resistor and capacitor). When the switch is closed, the current will begin to rise. If there were no inductor, the current would rise to a steady value of ξ/R, but the inductor will force a self-induced emf to appear in the circuit, and this will oppose the rise of the current. In other words, the resistor will e responding to two different emfs: the constant one created by the battery, and the variable one due to self-induction. With time, the rate at which the current increases will become less rapid, and the magnitude of the self-induced emf will decrease. At this point, the current in the circuit will approach ξ/R.

Mutual induction:

If two coils are placed next to one another, a steady current in one of the coils will set up a magnetic flux linking the other coil. If the current is changed in the first coil, an emf will appear in the second coil, in accordance with Faraday's law. Though we have generally referred to this process as induction, we might also call it mutual induction, to distinguish it from self-induction. A bit of math will show us that the emf induced in either coil is proportional to the rate of change of current in the other coil. We may then calculate the mutual induction for these two coils $\xi_2 = -M \frac{di_1}{dt}$ and $\xi_1 = -M \frac{di_2}{dt}$. The SI unit for induction is, of course, the henry.

Simple magnets

One of the most familiar physics demonstrations is the observation of the behavior of iron filings in the presence of a bar magnet. The pattern created by the filings will suggest that the magnet has two poles, where the magnetic field lines enter and leave. These poles are similar to the positive and negative charges of an electric dipole. Typically, we label these the north and south poles of the magnet; the north pole is the end from which the field lines emerge, and the south pole is the end into which they return. Any attempt to isolate these poles will be unsuccessful; that is, if the bar magnet is broken in half, new poles will form on the pieces of magnet. We will have to conclude that the simplest magnetic structure that can exist is a magnetic dipole. There are no magnetic monopoles.

Electrons:

There are three ways that electrons can generate magnetism. One way is by moving through an evacuated space or drifting through a conducting wire. Another is by its natural spinning motion. When an electron spins, its spin angular momentum is

$$S = \frac{h}{4\pi} = 5.2729 \times 10^{-35} J \cdot s$$
, where h is the Planck constant, the main constant in quantum physics. Magnetism that occurs at the subatomic level is typically measured in Bohr magnetons μ_B. Third and last, electrons generate magnetism through their orbits around the atomic nucleus. In fact, an orbiting electron is roughly equivalent to a tiny current loop.

Orbital angular momentum:

We may derive a clear relationship between the orbital magnetic moment of an electron and its orbital angular momentum. If we take an electron moving in a circular orbit of radius r and speed v, then we can calculate the magnetic dipole

moment $\mu_{orb} = \frac{e}{(2\pi r / v)} \pi r^2 = \frac{1}{2} evr$, and the angular momentum $L_{orb} = mvr$. Combined, these

equations in a vector formulation can be written: $\mu_{orb} = \frac{e}{2m} L_{orb}$. The negative sign is present because the orbiting electron is negatively charged. We will find that a Bohr magneton is equal to the orbital magnetic moment of an electron circulating in an orbit with the smallest allowed (nonzero) value of orbital angular momentum.

Gauss' law for magnetism:

Gauss' law for magnetism solidifies the assertion that magnetic monopoles cannot exist. The equation basically states that the net magnetic flux through a closed Gaussian surface must be zero: $\Phi_B = \oint B \cdot dA = 0$. Again, as with Gauss' law for electricity, we can say that the integral is to be taken over the entire Gaussian surface. If, for instance, we envision our Gaussian surface as enclosing one end of a short solenoid (which will set up a magnetic field resembling that of a magnetic dipole), we will notice that the magnetic field B will enter the Gaussian surface inside the solenoid (at the north pole) and will leave it outside the solenoid. No lines will begin or end in the surface, so the total flux for the surface is zero.

Magnetism of the earth:

The Earth functions as a giant magnet. Indeed, at points close to the earth, the magnetic field can be represented as the field of a bar magnet located at the center of the Earth. Generally, magnetic field lines emerge from the Earth's surface in the southern hemisphere and reenter it in the northern hemisphere, meaning that what we refer to as the Earth's north magnetic pole is actually the south pole of the Earth's magnetic dipole. The magnetic field of the Earth has many applications in navigation, communication, and prospecting. Most of the time, we are concerned with the field declination: that is, the angle between the true geographic north and the horizontal component of the magnetic field; and inclination, the angle between a horizontal plane and the field direction.

Paramagnetism:

Paramagnetism is a weaker and therefore less commonly-observed form of magnetism. Paramagnetism exists in atoms and ions in which the magnetic effects of the electrons do not cancel each other out, giving the atom as a whole a magnetic dipole moment μ.

Scientists will often measure the degree to which a sample of material is magnetized by dividing its measured magnetic moment by its volume. This vector quantity is known as the magnetization M of the sample. The SI unit for magnetization is the ampere-square meter per cubic meter. One important insight of paramagnetism is that the magnetization of a paramagnetic specimen is directly proportional to B, the effective magnetic field. This is known as Curie's law, and is written $M = C\left(\dfrac{B}{T}\right)$, in which C is Curie's constant.

Ferromagnetism:

Ferromagnetism is the form of magnetism with which most of us are familiar. It is caused by a special interaction known as exchange coupling. In this process, the atomic dipoles of particular elements may be aligned in a very rigid parallel structure, despite the fact that thermal motions tends to send these magnetic dipoles into random patterns. This holds true for iron, nickel, cobalt, and other substances. Experiments have shown that if the temperature is raised above a certain temperature, known as the Curie temperature, exchanging coupling ceases. In order to study the magnetization of a ferromagnetic substance, physicists usually form it into a toroid. Physicists will then plot a so-called magnetization curve, on which the ratio between magnetism created by a current through the toroid and ferromagnetism.

Alternating current circuits

When we say that something is wired for alternating current (ac), we mean that the current value will vary over time in a sinusoidal fashion. Most often, the alternating current of a home or office will change direction 120 times every second. This may seem counterproductive to producing a constant current, but we should remember that current is created simply by the motion of charge carriers, not necessarily by continuous motion in one direction. The advantage of an alternating current is that it creates the constant change in current creates a magnetic field. It also makes it possible for us to adjust the potential difference with a device called a transformer. Alternating currents and the subsequent alternating emfs are essential to television, radio, and most modern electronics.

Resistive circuits:

Let us imagine a simple circuit with a current generator and some resistive element. The alternating emf of the current generator is $\xi = \xi_m \sin \omega t$. Because the amplitude of the alternating potential difference (or voltage) across the resistor is equal to the amplitude of the alternating emf, we may say $v_R = V_R \sin \omega t$. Using our definition of resistance, we may also say that $i_R = \dfrac{v_R}{R} = \dfrac{V_R}{R} \sin \omega t = I_R \sin \omega t$. Here, though, since we are dealing with a purely resistive load, we may say that the phase constant $\phi = 0^o$, and so the voltage amplitude and current amplitude are related: $V_R = I_R R$.

Capacitive circuits:

Let us imagine a simple circuit containing a capacitor and a generator with alternating emf $\xi = \xi_m \sin \omega t$. Using the loop rule, we may say that the potential difference across the capacitor is $v_c = V_c \sin \omega t$, in which V_c is the voltage amplitude across the capacitor. In order to outline the relation between voltage amplitude and current amplitude, we will introduce the quantity X_c, which is known as the capacitive reactance of the capacitor and is defined: $X_C = \dfrac{1}{\omega C}$. This value depends in part on the angular frequency at which the capacitor is operating. The SI unit for C is the second per ohm. Incorporating this quantity, we can find the equation for the relation between voltage amplitude and current amplitude: $V_c = I_c X_c$.

Inductive circuit:

Let us imagine a simple circuit composed of an inductor and a generator with alternating emf $\xi = \xi_m \sin \omega t$. Using the loop rule, we may say $v_L = V_L \sin \omega t$, where V_L is the voltage amplitude across the inductor. In order to consider the relation between the current amplitude and the voltage amplitude, we must introduce the concept of inductive reactance

X_L, such that $X_L = \omega L$. The SI unit of inductive reactance is the ohm. We can use the measure for inductive reactance to establish the relation between current amplitude and voltage amplitude: $V_L = I_L X_L$. This equation will hold up for any alternating current circuit, no matter how complicated.

Transformers

For an alternating-current circuit, the average rate of energy dissipation in a resistive load is given by the equation: $P_{av} = IV$, where a given power requirement is met by some combination of current and potential difference. In electric power distribution systems, like appliances, it makes sense to have a low potential difference in order to maintain safety. In systems that transmit energy, however, it may be more desirable to have a low current and a high potential difference, because this will minimize losses during transmission. Indeed, if energy companies were to transmit electricity at a high current, they would lose over half of the electricity they sent! For this reason, energy suppliers strive to transmit at the highest possible voltage and the lowest possible current.

Ideal transformer:

Because energy companies want to transmit electricity with the highest possible voltage and the lowest possible current, they need a device to adjust potential difference while keeping the product of voltage multiplied by current at a constant. The device that is used to accomplish this feat is called a transformer. If we were to imagine an ideal transformer, it would have two coils wound around an iron core. The first winding is connected to an alternating-current generator. The second winding is connected to a resistor, though it can be made into an open circuit by flipping a switch. We will assume that no energy escapes this transformer due to any resistances in the windings.

Having set up our ideal transformer, we see that the primary coil will act almost purely as an inductor, and will create a small magnetizing current. At the same time, an alternating magnetic flux will be created in the iron core. And, because this core extends through the

- 120 -

secondary windings, so will the induced flux. The voltage in each of the two circuits will be

$$V_s = V_p \left(\frac{N_s}{N_p} \right)$$. If $N_s \succ N_p$, then the transformer is called a step-up transformer, because it

increases the voltage; if $N_s \prec N_p$, then the voltage is decreased and the transformer is

known as a step-down transformer. If we then close the switch for the second coil, an

alternating current appear that is just big enough to cancel the opposing emf generated by

the primary windings. This relation can be expressed $$I_s = I_p \left(\frac{N_p}{N_s} \right)$$ for the transformation of

currents, and $$R_{eq} = \left(\frac{N_p}{N_s} \right)^2 R$$ for the transformation of resistances.

Impedance matching:

If we look at the equation for the transformation of resistances, $$R_{eq} = \left(\frac{N_p}{N_s} \right)^2 R$$, we can detect

another possible use for the transformer. In order for there to be a maximum transfer of

energy from an emf device to a resistive load, the resistance of the device and the

resistance of the load must be equal. This same relation will hold up for ac circuits, except

instead of resistance, the impedance of the generator must be matched to the resistance of

the load. Oftentimes, the impedances of two different devices will be quite different; as in

the case of a speaker set and amplifier, for instance. In such cases, the impedances can be

matched by coupling them through a transformer with a suitable turns ratio N_p / N_s.

And discuss Lorentz force law

The Lorentz force law describes the force exerted on a charged particle in an

electromagnetic field. The force exerted on the particle can be found $F = q(E + v \times B)$,

where the terms on the right side of the equation are electric charge (of the particle),

electric field, velocity, and magnetic field, respectively. Essentially, this law states that a

positively charged particle will be accelerated in the same linear direction as the electric field, but will curve perpendicularly to the magnetic field according to the right-hand rule. The Lorentz force law is used in a number of devices currently employed by physicists, like the cyclotron, magnetron, mass spectrometer, motor, generator, and rail gun.

Important terms

Electron configuration - a description of how an atom's electrons are distributed through its energy levels and sub-levels. The energy level, sub-level, and number of electrons are represented with numbers and letters. For example, H has one electron in one energy level; its electron configuration is represented thus: $1s^2$. More complex atoms with higher atomic numbers have more complex configurations and notations, but the configuration is predictable based on the element's location on the periodic table.

Ionization energy - the energy required to separate electrons from their atoms, creating ions. Electrons will not separate from the atoms to which they are bound without some force acting upon them. Ionization energy is one of the trends exhibited in the periodic table; it decreases reading from top to bottom within a group, and increases reading from left to right within a period.

Rate laws - the relationship between concentration of reactants and reaction rate. The relative speed of a reaction may increase with changes in reactant amounts; it may also decrease or show no impact. Rate laws track the effects of changes in reactant concentration on reaction rates.

First order reactions - those reactions in which only a single reactant has an impact on reaction rate. The rate increases or decreases in direct proportion to the concentration of the reactant: doubling the concentration of reactant doubles the rate.

Second order reactions - those in which both reactants impact the rate of reaction, and the relationship is not proportional, but exponential: doubling a reactant concentration raises the rate by four.

Zero order reactions - reactions in which changes in reactant concentration had no effect on reaction rate.

Ligand - an atom or group of atoms which bonds to a central atom in reactions, assuming a central atom can be determined. They sometimes cannot.

Bridging ligand - a ligand that connects two or more atoms or parts of the structure; these usually serve to bridge between two metallic atoms due to the ionic bonding propensities of metals.

Chelation - the formation of bonds or intramolecular attractions on specific binding sites within ligands. .

Leaving group - an atom or group that detaches from another atom or group in a given reaction.

Entering group - an atom or group which forms bonds with an existing atom or group of any given reaction. Groups can enter or leave on both sides of the reaction equation.

Exothermic reactions - chemical reactions in which energy is released or produced, as in combustion.

Endothermic reactions – reactions which require external energy for the reaction to occur, and is absorbed from the surroundings.

Activation energy - some reactions require energy to start the reaction; this energy is called activation energy. A match applied to tissue paper is an example of activation energy.

Reaction equilibrium - When the same number of atoms is present on the reactant side of an equation as on the product side, the reaction is said to be in equilibrium. All atoms of a substance must be accounted for after it undergoes a chemical reaction. For instance, methane reacting with oxygen produces water and carbon dioxide, but all atoms in the original substances are still present, albeit in different combinations.

Transition state - the point of highest energy during a chemical reaction. Reactions exhibit differing energies—or enthalpies—as a reaction progresses; these differences are plotted as a curve in "reaction coordinate diagrams" and are one way of tracing reaction rate. The transition state is the highest point on the plotted curve.

Intermediate - a state of matter produced during a reaction that is neither reactant nor product, but something intermediary. They are typically highly unstable and exist for only a short time before becoming product.

Concerted reactions - reactions in bonds break and form simultaneously with no time interval or intermediates.

Multi-step reactions - require several steps to complete and often involve intermediates and enzymes, and may also depend on the polarity of the solution.

Oxidizing agent - the reactant in oxidation reactions which gains electrons, causing oxidation of the other reactant(s). Peroxides, iodine and other halogens, and sulfoxides are common oxidizing agents.

Reduction agent – (or reducing agent) is the reactant oxidized in an oxidation reaction; it loses electrons to the oxidizing agent. In rusting iron, a common oxidation reaction, iron is the reducing agent, losing electrons to oxygen.

Rate-determining step - in multi-step reactions, each of the steps have different reaction rates—often very different. The rate-determining step is the slowest portion of such reactions. Because the reaction can only go as fast as its slowest step, that step determines overall reaction rate.

Electrophile - the acceptor of an electron pair in chemical reactions. A cation "seeks" additional electrons to balance its negative charge, so is an electrophile.

Nucleophiles - donors of electron pairs in reactions. Anions are nucleophilic because they "seek" a positively charged region near a nucleus to balance their negative charges.

Pericyclic reactions - reactions whose defining characteristic is the reorganization of π and σ bonds through cyclic transition states. There are no intermediates in these reactions because electrons shift during the transition state to transform reactant immediately to product. Or in other words, the molecular orbitals of the reactant are transformed into the molecular orbitals of the product. Pericyclic reactions require activation energy, though not necessarily a great deal.

Electrocyclic reactions - a class of exothermic pericyclic reaction in which a cyclic reactant is transformed into another cyclic product with one less double bond than the reactant.

Cyclic compounds - hydrocarbons whose bonding structure creates ring-shaped molecules. Hydrocarbons also occur in the form of long chains.

Amino acids - the building blocks of peptides and proteins. They are carboxylic acids with an amino group ($-NH_2$) bonded to the carboxyl group. Common amino acids include glycine, cystine, tryptophan, and phenylalanine.

Carbon tetravalency - the tendency of carbon atoms to form four covalent bonds with other atoms in organic compounds. This predictability is important because all organic compounds contain carbon. Its tetravalency, due to its four valence electrons, enables inferences and predictions about properties and reactions of organic compounds.

Benzene- C_6H_6, is an important cyclic compound in organic chemistry which forms the backbone of many other compounds when H bound to the ring's C is replaced by other groups or elements.

Aromatic compounds - compounds with benzene as a base. Many of them have strong odors.

Alkoxy (or alkoxyl) group - any group and an oxygen atom attached to an ether. It can react with hydrogen to form an alcohol.

Dehydration - a very important reaction involving alcohols in which H and O atoms are removed as H2O product. It is an elimination reaction because two or more covalent bonds are broken in a single alcohol molecule and a C=C bond is formed in the product, forming an alkene. If two or more alcohol molecules are involved in the dehydration reaction, an ether is the product.

Denatured alcohol - Ethanol (CH3CH2OH) is the alcohol in alcoholic beverages and is a product of fermentation. Other substances are sometimes added to ethanol to make it unfit for drinking; such altered ethanol is called denatured alcohol.

Primary, secondary, and tertiary alcohols - are those in which the alkoxy group (–OH) is bonded to the primary, secondary, or tertiary C atoms, respectively.

Acetal - a product of an aldehyde's reaction with an alcohol and is an important compound in carbohydrate chemistry.

Hemiacetals - unstable intermediates on their way to becoming acetals; their transformation is completed in the presence of an acid catalyst.

Ketals - products of a ketone's reaction with alcohol.

Hemiketals - the intermediates in such reactions and are very unstable.

Benedict's reagent - an important component of experiments involving aldehydes. It is a solution with mild oxidizing properties containing Cu^{2+} ions and produces a red precipitate in the presence of aldehydes.

Tollen's reagent - used for similar purposes but contains silver ions instead of copper. In the presence of aldehydes, the silver in solution precipitates to form solid silver.

Aldol condensation - a reaction in which two aldehyde molecules join to form a product called an aldol containing both aldehyde and alcohol functional groups. It is an important reaction in several industrial processes such as the production of insect repellent.

Diels-Alder reaction - a cycloaddition reaction in which two unsaturated hydrocarbons combine to form a ring. It involves a conjugated diene (an unsaturated hydrocarbon with two C=C double bonds) and either an alkene or alkyne. The two terminal atoms of the diene bond to the C atoms of the alkene double bond to form a ring with five C—C bonds and one C=C bond; the double bond of the former diene remains while the double bonds of the alkene are "lost." These reactions are stereospecific: they occur only with specific isomeric configurations.

Science Learning, Instruction, and Assessment

Independent practice

Independent practice occurs when skills and strategies have been taught in the classroom as a part of a unit or activity. Practice follows once an activity has been set and the teacher has observed the students independently working in order to judge whether or not the skill has been learned. Independent practice takes place when new skills are to be applied in familiar formats and judges whether or not students are able to apply new information. For example, if students are learning about division, the teacher may teach long division by starting out with smaller numbers, and then give the students problems that contain more numbers than taught to see if they are able to apply the information effectively.

Homework

Homework is generally the time that students spend outside of the classroom completing assigned activities that practices, reviews or applies skills learned in the classroom. It enables students to work independently therefore improving independent study skills. Homework can provide more practice time for tasks that students find challenging and extend the knowledge of students who have already grasped the material. It can assist teachers in knowing how the students are progressing with the material, and help them to help students who are struggling. If students are held accountable for the work they do, it helps them to become more responsible and accountable for their work. It can also be a time to engage the parents in the work and encourage parents to take part in their students' education, as well as knowing that the school has high expectations for each student.

Teacher's role:

Homework should never be seen as a punishment, so giving students "no homework" as a reward should be avoided. Make sure that the homework assignments are varied by having some be short term and others being long term. Having homework assignments that take too long to be completed should be avoided so that students don't see homework as a constant frustration. If links are made to class work and homework, then students will see homework as important to the class and do it more regularly. Instructions should be clear as well as the consequences for late or incomplete homework. It should be corrected in a timely manner so that students will be able to track their progress and should also include feedback so students will know how they can improve.

Role of parents:

At the beginning of the year, it is helpful to have a handout for parents on the expectations in the classroom, as well as with homework. This way they will know what is to be expected and can assist their children as needed. Also including some tips as how to set up a good study environment and ways for the parent to help with the homework can be good things to include as well. When the first instances of incomplete or late homework occur, it is important to contact parents as soon as necessary so that the parents will realize that homework is important to the class. Having a homework diary or some place, like in the back of a notebook, where the students keep a list of homework can help parents know what is expected of their children and enable to help them accordingly.

Transitions

Transitions are periods of time in which the activity moves from one stage to another. It could be the time period between when a teacher assigns a task to when the students actually start the task, or the time period between when the students enter the room and when they are sitting at their desks. Successful transitions require many things, including careful planning, teaching, monitoring and feedback. How to deal with transitions needs to be taught to the students just as any other classroom routine. For example, having a list of things for students to do after they finish a task before the other students do can stop problems with behavior if they always know that there is something for them to do. Most students will respond well to knowing the structures for transitions, especially since there are so many on a daily basis that they will encounter.

Improving students' transition skills:

Setting teaching routines is an important way to teach transition skills because it lets the students know what is expected of them. By modeling both incorrect and correct examples of what to do, the students can see clearly what is expected. Also, making sure that the teacher reminds students what to do before the transition occurs will refresh their memory and give them a chance to succeed. Although it is important not to do this all the time, otherwise students will always expect to have a warning instead of just sensing the transition. When students to engage in appropriate behavior, having incentives and specific praise should be given. By recognizing appropriate behavior and ignoring or directing inappropriate behavior, students will know what to do. Finally, by having the teacher actively scanning the classroom, and moving around, students will feel the need to stay on task because they know they are being monitored.

Problem solving

Problem solving is an important skill that is used in all classes. The best way to initiate the cycle of problem solving is to ask questions that will spur students into a dialogue about the problem which will work out how they will begin to attempt the task. If they know what the problem is first, and having students define everything they know about the task, then they will be better suited to attempt to solve it. If they are able to visualize or imagine the solution, then their experimentation toward the means will have more purpose as they can see what they are working towards. It students are having trouble moving on, or are stuck, encourage them to take a break, by walking around if appropriate, or not looking at the material. Once a solution is found, have the students write down as much as they can in order to avoid other complications that could appear while planning the solution.

Assessment

Strategies:

An assessment is an illustrative task or opportunity to perform that targets the educational objectives for an assignment and allows students to demonstrate what they have learned and the progress of their learning. There are many strategies that can be used as strategies to assess student learning. Graphic organizers can allow the presentation of a variety of information or show how the information was obtained and learned. Interviewing others can provide a real life experience to a topic studied in class and put a face to the story and experience. Doing an observation can help students see how the topic appears in real life. If students complete self or peer evaluations, these can be useful because sometimes feedback from a peer group is more valuable than that of a teacher. Finally, portfolios can contain a little bit of everything and can track how the students have progressed through the assessment.

Rubrics:

Assessment rubrics are authentic assessment tools that are used to measure the work of students. It aims to evaluate a student's performance based on a set of criteria related to the task, rather than giving a single score for the work. Students usually receive the rubric before they attempt the task so that they know what is expected and for them to think about how the criteria will play out in their work. They can be analytic or holistic and are tailored to individual assessment tasks, allowing teachers to design the rubric for individual classes and the needs of the students. Rubrics are also a formative type of assessment because it is an ongoing part of the teaching and learning process since it is revealed to the students before the assessment is even commenced.

Standard error of measurement:

Standard error of measurement - The estimate of the 'error' associated with the test-taker's obtained score when compared with their hypothetical 'true' score. The SEM, which varies from test to test, should be given in the test manual. The band of scores in which we can be fairly certain the 'true' score lies can be calculated from this figure.

Standard deviation:

A measure of the range of values in a set of numbers. Standard deviation is a statistic used as a measure of the dispersion or variation in a distribution, equal to the square root of the arithmetic mean of the squares of the deviations from the arithmetic mean.

The standard deviation of a random variable or list of numbers (the lowercase greek sigma) is the square of the variance. The standard deviation of the list x1, x2, x3...xn with mean μ is given by the formula:

$$\sigma = \sqrt{\frac{(x_1 - \mu)^2 + (x_2 - \mu)^2 + \cdots + (x_n - \mu)^2}{n}}$$

The formula is used when all of the values in the population are known. If the values x1...xn are a random sample chosen from the population, then the sample Standard Deviation is calculated with same formula, except that (n-1) is used as the denominator.

Scores:

Grade equivalent score - how typical students at the grade level specified would perform on the test that has been given. In other words, the grade equivalent of 10.4 does not indicate that the 4th grade is doing of doing 10th grade work. Rather, it indicates that the 4th grade student has performed as well as a typical 10th grade student would have performed on the 4th grade test. If the student is performing on grade level, that is a 4th grade student taking the test in the 10th month of 4th grade receives a score of 4.10, then it simply indicates that he/she is performing right at the average for other 4th graders in the norming sample, which is the 50th percentile and 50th NCE. Grade equivalents do not lend themselves to measuring aggregate performance of all students in a school or school district. They do not average well and are hard to understand when dealing with groups. Accordingly, the score used in this study is the Normal Curve Equivalent, or NCE.

Raw score - is an original datum that has not been transformed. A standard score is a dimensionless quantity derived from the raw score

Scaled score - is a standardized score, that is, it is based on the normal distribution and standard deviation units.

Mastery levels - The cutoff score on a criterion-referenced or mastery test; people who score at or above the cutoff score are considered to have mastered the material; mastery may be an arbitrary judgment.

Communication

Effective communication techniques :

Two main ways to ensure general effective communication techniques involve listening actively and the nonverbal message that is being sent to the speaker.

- When listening, remain attentive and concentrate on what is being said. Also, don't form an opinion right away, be impartial in order to take the most away from what is being said. Reflecting on what is being said can be done by restating the message so that the speaker knows that you understand. Summarizing what the speaker has said will also show that you have paid attention to the details.

- The nonverbal message conveyed is also important. You should be aware of your body posture and the level of eye contact you are using. Staring them straight in the eye could be seen as confrontational, whereas complete lack of eye contact can be viewed as disinterest. If you are speaking to a student, try to have a parallel body position, either both be standing or sitting in order to put you both on an equal level.

Motivating students:

Repeating keys terms or concepts frequently is preferential. The more times students hear something, the more likely they will be to remember it later. Thus, reviewing key concepts often is going to be most effective. Providing students with visual aids to reinforce and explain abstract concepts is going to be more important as today's students tend to be visual learners. Encourage students to use logical thinking when necessary by pointing out which information is fact and which exists logically. This will help students apply knowledge in new situations more readily. By using in-class activities to reinforce newly presented materials will allow students to show what they have learned. Having students give feedback about what they have learned will also increase their understanding.

Assist students by creating a link when you are teaching something new. If students can see how it relates to something that they have previously taught, then the odds of learning the new material are increased. Vocabulary is something to be considered, both what the teacher uses and what the students use. It should be introduced with a real-life definition and with many opportunities for the students to use the words. Students should be communicated with in respect and addressed appropriately for the setting in order for them to reciprocate respect. Finally, communicating that students are held to high standards right from the start will let them know what is to be expected and for them to keep striving for their best.

Factors affecting communication:
- Ethnocentrism: The inability to accept another culture's world view.
- Discrimination: Treatment of an individual that is differential due to minority status, whether actual or perceived.
- Stereotyping: Generalizing how a person is to be treated, while ignoring the fact that individual differences occur.
- Cultural Blindness: Differences in culture or language are ignored as though the differences did not exist.

- Cultural imposition: The belief that everyone should conform to the majority.

Cultural differences:

The cultural differences that might affect behavior include: eye contact, hand movements, silence, religious belief and loss of face. It is important to know the differences that some students may have with eye contact, for example, in some cultures, looking down is seen as a sign of respect, whereas with some students that is the way to show respect and that they are paying attention. Some students may laugh or smile out of nervousness when under pressure, falsely leading teachers to assume that they are being rude or misbehaving. Silence is one that varies between genders and cultures. Girls tend to be quieter, and students who are silent when called upon, could actually be waiting for more direction instead of the impression that they are not paying attention. Religious beliefs come into effect when doing particular activities that certain religions would find inappropriate, therefore causing students to be reluctant to participate, not because they don't know what to do but because they can't do the activity.

Nonverbal communication

Nonverbal communication is all the ways in which humans send and receive messages without using words to communicate them. For teachers, it is just important to be effective nonverbal communicators as well as verbal communicators. They are essential aspects of the teaching process and can sometimes even be more effective than a verbal reminder. Nonverbal communication includes gestures, facial expressions, proximity, humor, posture, body orientation or touching. Being aware of the ways the students communicate nonverbally can also assist teachers in getting messages about how their students are learning. Sometimes sending signals can reinforce learning more effectively, because they are implicit and students will learn how to react to your nonverbal communication more readily because it tends to be less confrontational than direct statements.

Important kinds of nonverbal communication:

Four commonly used types of nonverbal communication are eye contact, facial expressions, gestures, and body orientation.

- Eye contact helps to regulate the flow of communication between two people as well as registering interest in the topic at hand. Teachers who use eye contact convey warmth, concern and directness.
- Facial expressions are nonverbal communicators that have been taught to us since birth to convey a wide range of emotions. For instance, smiling conveys happiness, warmth, friendless and liking. If teachers smile often, then students will tend to react positively and develop a good feeling toward the class and sometimes even learn more.
- Gestures can include movements with hands that sometimes serve no larger purpose than entertainment or to keep attention.
- Body orientation gets across the message that you are either interested or disinterested in the person speaking to you; leaning forward is more favorable of a position then reclining back in your chair.

Nonverbal communication techniques:

Three more aspects of nonverbal communication include proximity, paralinguistics and humor.

- Proximity is usually set out by the cultural norms regarding space. When a student is not focusing, sometimes just standing next to his desk is just as effective as verbally reminding him to pay attention. Usually having the teacher walk around the room increases interaction with the students.
- Paralinguistics is the vocal elements of nonverbal communication, such as tone, pitch, rhythm, loudness and inflection. Teachers who speak in a monotone voice tend to be perceived as boring because there is no variety. But, when teachers use variety in their voice, it tends to keep the interest of the students longer.

- Humor can also be a useful teaching tool because it can release stress and tension for both the teacher and students. It can foster a friendly classroom environment that facilitates learning, and as long as it is used appropriately, is very useful and effective.

Choosing course content

Texts and reading should be chosen whose language is gender-neutral and free of stereotypes, and texts that do include these should be addressed and discussed. The curriculum should be inclusive by including the perspectives and experiences of a pluralistic society. All points of view should be presented so that no one view takes precedence over the others. When making references to culture or history, make sure that your students are either given background information or the opportunities to ask for clarification. Do not assume that all of you students will be able to pick up on these references. Considering students needs when assigning homework is also considerate based on the different family structures at home. If requiring the use of a computer, make sure that opportunities to use computers at school are permitted in the case of students who do not have access to one at home.

Gender-neutral language:
Gender neutral language is language that attempts to not refer to either a male or female when coming up with an example where the sex of the person involved cannot be determined. For example, when teaching occupations, making sure that all occupations are either male or female, depend on the word chosen, like chair instead of chairman. It is preferable to avoid regendering terms, therefore chair is preferable to chairwoman if the person being referred to is a woman. Creating gender neutral terms is also effective, for example adding is to adjectives to avoid specifying which sex the person is. Also, avoiding terms that have –ette and –ess endings are good because those tend to be derogatory.

Community

A caring community is the way that the school interacts with the surrounding neighborhood and town. All families are welcome in the school and the immediate area is seen in the spirit of cooperation between the students and their families. The populations of students that attend a school will tend to be diverse, therefore all families should feel included in the community of the school. Individual students will feel included if they are treated well by the staff and their fellow students and feel that the staff has concern for their well being, and that they are valued. In order for this to work, students must feel that their input and participation is a necessary function of the school and that there is communication between all facets of the school and the community. Family and staff members work together to solve problems and the rights of all students are strictly upheld.

Setting up community in the classroom:

By setting up the environment in the classroom from the beginning means that put downs are eliminated so that students feel safe in the environment. Students should treat the teacher with courtesy and respect, and that should be reciprocated. Having interactions between students on a regular basis will increase the level of community in the classroom because students will get to know each other and not use prejudice readily. When appropriate, if the students have the chance to put their input into what they study, then they will feel motivated to learn and share their knowledge with others. Balancing between teacher-centered and student-centered activities will spread out the activities and make students feel accountable for their own learning. Setting an appropriate way to deal with behavior will also increase the sense of community if students feel that they are being dealt with appropriately as well as seeing other students dealt with for misbehaving on a regular basis.

Divergent thinking

Divergent thinking is generating many ideas about a topic in a short period of time. It stems from the idea that there isn't one right idea, but that many ideas are possible. It involves taking one topic and breaking it down into many smaller parts in order to gain insight about the topic as a whole. Divergent thinking usually occurs in spontaneous, free-flowing ways because the ideas that create this type of thinking often are thought of in these patterns as well. The ideas may then be put back together in a more structured way in order to be understandable to the other students. It can be an effective way for students to start a new topic as divergent thinking will allow them to examine what they already know about the topic.

Stimulating divergent thinking:

Two ways to stimulate divergent thinking are brainstorming and keeping a journal. Brainstorming involves making a list of ideas in a creative, yet unstructured way. Its goal is to generate as many ideas in a short period of time. It often relies on one idea to spawn the process of thinking in a variety of directions. During brainstorming, all ideas are seen as important and no idea is disregarded or criticized. They are all seen as important because of the thought process. After brainstorming is complete, only then can the list be reviewed and the best ideas sorted out from the rest. Keeping a journal is also an effective way to record ideas that one thinks of on a daily basis. It can take the form of a small notebook, or just a piece of paper on which to jot ideas. This is useful because students sometimes will gather inspiration at unusual times and places, and by always having a journal handy, it can be ensured that the ideas don't go to waste.

Free writing and mind or subject mapping are two others ways that can stimulate divergent thinking. Free writing is when a student focuses on one particular topic and writes non-stop about it for a short period of time. It could be on an idea that was spawned during brainstorming, or on a new unit in a class. It is useful to generate a variety of thought on a topic that can then be used for later work in the unit once it is restructured or put into a logical order. Finally, mind or subject mapping involves taking all the brainstormed ideas and putting them into a visual organizer that shows the relationship between the ideas. It may start with a central theme, and then show all the topics related to the theme and their subtopics.

Convergent thinking

Convergent thinking is that which represents the analysis or integration of already taught or previous knowledge. It leads you to an expected end result or answer. It usually involves the terms explaining, stating relationships, and comparing and contrasting. The way it is structured may differ, but the expected result will be a justified answer to the topic. Questions to stir up convergent thinking usually begin with why, how or in what ways. These ensure that the thinking is led in a certain direction with the answer always in mind. Using these question tags effectively will require specific events or people so that the students know what the expected answer should involve.

IEP

Special education teachers help to develop an Individualized Education Program (IEP) for each special education student. The IEP sets personalized goals for each student and is tailored to the student's individual needs and ability. When appropriate, the program includes a transition plan outlining specific steps to prepare students with disabilities for middle school or high school or, in the case of older students, a job or postsecondary study. Teachers review the IEP with the student's parents, school administrators, and the student's general education teacher. Teachers work closely with parents to inform them of their child's progress and suggest techniques to promote learning at home.

Inappropriate treatment of students

According to the U.S. Children's Bureau, "More than half (approximately 53%) of all reports alleging maltreatment came from professionals, including educators, law enforcement and justice officials, medical and mental health professionals, social service professionals, and child care providers."

David Finkelhor, Director of the Crimes Against Children Research Center and Codirector of the Family Research Laboratory at the University of New Hampshire says, "The key problem is educators are confused about what child protection does and whether it does any good." Finkelhor, who has been studying child victimization, child maltreatment, and family violence since 1977, adds, "There is the other problem that schools may not support the reporting process."

Individuals with Disabilities Education Act

The Individuals with Disabilities Education Act (IDEA) is the law that guarantees all children with disabilities access to a free and appropriate public education.

Practice Test

Multiple Choice Questions

1. Which substance is most likely to be a solid at STP?
    a. Kr
    b. Na
    c. NH_3
    d. Xe

2. Which of the following tend to increase the melting point of a solid?
    I. Increasing molecular weight
    II. Decreasing polarity
    III. Increasing surface area
    a. I and II
    b. II
    c. III
    d. I and III

3. A gas at constant volume is cooled. Which statement about the gas must be true?
    a. The kinetic energy of the gas molecules has decreased.
    b. The gas has condensed to a liquid.
    c. The weight of the gas has decreased.
    d. The density of the gas has increased.

4. A weather balloon is filled with 1000 mol of He gas at 25 °C and 101 kPa of pressure. What is the volume of the weather balloon?
    a. 24518 m3
    b. 24.5 m3
    c. 2 m3
    d. 245 m³

5. One mole of oxygen gas and two moles of hydrogen are combined in a sealed container at STP. Which of the following statements is true?
    a. The mass of hydrogen gas is greater than the mass of oxygen.
    b. The volume of hydrogen is greater than the volume of oxygen.
    c. The hydrogen and oxygen will react to produce 2 mol of water.
    d. The partial pressure of hydrogen is greater than the partial pressure of oxygen.

6. Graham's law is best used to determine what relationship between two different materials?
    a. pressure and volume
    b. volume and temperature
    c. mass and diffusion rate
    d. Diffusion rate and temperature

7. Which is the correct order of increasing intermolecular attractive forces?
    a. Dipole-dipole<ionic<hydrogen bonding<London dispersion
    b. Ionic<dipole-dipole<London dispersion<hydrogen bonding
    c. Hydrogen bonding<London dispersion<ionic<dipole-dipole
    d. London dispersion<dipole-dipole<hydrogen bonding<ionic

8. One mole of an ideal gas is compressed to 10 L and heated to 25 °C. What is the pressure of the gas?
    a. 2.4 KPa
    b. 2.4 atm
    c. 0.2 atm
    d. 0.2 KPa

9. A 10 L cylinder contains 4 moles of oxygen, 3 moles of nitrogen and 7 moles of neon. The temperature of the cylinder is increased from 20 °C to 40 °C. Determine the partial pressure of neon in the cylinder as a percentage of the whole.
    a. 50%
    b. 70%
    c. 90%
    d. 40%

10. Three liquids, X, Y and Z are placed in separate flasks, each of which is suspended in a water bath at 75 °C. The boiling points of each liquid are
        X, 273 K
        Y, 340 K
        Z, 360 K
Which of the three liquids will begin to boil after warming to 75 °C?
    a. X, Y, and Z
    b. X and Z
    c. X and Y
    d. Y and Z

11. Which of the following statements is true about the physical properties of liquids and gases?
        I. Liquids and gases are both compressible
        II. Liquids flow, but gases do not
        III. Liquids flow, and gases are incompressible
        IV. Liquids flow and gases are compressible
        V. Gases flow and liquids are incompressible
    a. I and III
    b. II and IV
    c. III and V
    d. IV and V

12. Which of the following statements **generally** describes the trend of electronegativity considering the Periodic Table of the Elements?
    a. Electronegativity increases going from left to right and from top to bottom
    b. Electronegativity increases going from right to left and from bottom to top
    c. Electronegativity increases going from left to right and from bottom to top
    d. Electronegativity increases going from right to left and from top to bottom

13. Gas X is in a cylinder at 1 atm of pressure and has a volume of 10 L at 0° C. Gas X spontaneously decomposes to gas Y, according to the equation

$$X \longrightarrow 3Y$$

The temperature in the cylinder remains the same during the reaction. What is the pressure in the cylinder now?
    a. 1 atm
    b. 3 atm
    c. 4 atm
    d. Cannot be determined

14. 1 mole of water and 1 mole of argon are in a cylinder at 110 °C and 1 atm of pressure. The temperature of the cylinder is reduced to -5 °C. Which statement about the contents of the cylinder is most accurate?
    a. The pressure in the cylinder is decreased, and the partial pressure of argon is less than that of water.
    b. The pressure in the cylinder is about the same, and the partial pressure of water is less than that of argon.
    c. The pressure in the cylinder is decreased, and the partial pressure of water is much less than that of argon.
    d. The pressure in the cylinder is decreased and the partial pressure of water is the same as argon.

15. A solid is heated until it melts. Which of the following is true about the solid melting?
    a. ΔH is positive, and ΔS is positive
    b. ΔH is negative and ΔS is positive
    c. ΔH is positive and ΔS is negative
    d. ΔH is negative and ΔS is negative

16. A liquid is held at its freezing point and slowly allowed to solidify. Which of the following statements about this event are true?
    a. During freezing, the temperature of the material decreases
    b. While freezing, heat is given off by the material
    c. During freezing, heat is absorbed by the material
    d. During freezing, the temperature of the material increases

17. A liquid is heated from 50 °C to 80 °C. Which of the following statements is generally true about the solubility of solids and gases in the liquid?
    a. The solubility of solids will increase and the solubility of gases will decrease
    b. The solubility of solids will decrease and the solubility of gases will increase
    c. The solubility of solids will increase and the solubility of gases will increase
    d. The solubility of solids will decrease and the solubility of gases will decrease

18. 100 g of H_3PO_4 is dissolved in water, producing 400 mL of solution. What is the normality of the solution?
    a. 2.55 N
    b. 1.02 N
    c. 7.65 N
    d. 0.25 N

19. Silver nitrate ($AgNO_3$) is dissolved in water. One drop of an aqueous solution containing NaCl is added and almost instantly, a white milky precipitate forms. What is the precipitate?
   a. NaCl
   b. $NaNO_3$
   c. $AgNO_3$
   d. AgCl

20. 100 g of ethanol C_2H_6O is dissolved in 100 g of water. The final solution has a volume of 0.2 L. What is the density of the resulting solution?
   a. 0.5 g/mL
   b. 1 g/mL
   c. 46 g/mL
   d. 40 g/mL

21. 100 mL of a 0.1 M solution of NaOH is neutralized to pH 7 with H_2SO_4. How many grams of H_2SO_4 are required to achieve this neutralization?
   a. 4.9 g
   b. 0.98 g
   c. 9.8 g
   d. 0.49 g

22. Comparing pure water and a 1 M aqueous solution of NaCl, both at 1 atm of pressure, which of the following statements is most accurate?
   a. The pure water will boil at a higher temperature, and be less conductive
   b. The pure water will boil at a lower temperature and be less conductive
   c. The pure water will boil at a lower temperature and be more conductive
   d. The pure water boil at the same temperature and be more conductive

23. Place the following in the correct order of increasing acidity.
   a. HCl<HF<HI<HBr
   b. HCl<HBr<HI<HF
   c. HI<HBr<HCl<HF
   d. HF<HCl<HBr<HI

24. Place the following in the correct order of increasing solubility in water.
   a. Butanol<ethanol<octane<NaCl
   b. Ethanol<NaCl<octane<butanol
   c. NaCl<octane<butanol<ethanol
   d. Octane<butanol<ethanol<NaCl

25. 50 grams of acetic acid $C_2H_4O_2$ are dissolved in 200 g of water. Calculate the weight % and mole fraction of the acetic acid in the solution.
   a. 20%, 0.069
   b. 0.069%, 0.20
   c. 25%, 0.075
   d. 20%, 0.075

26. Ammonium Phosphate $(NH_4)_3PO_4$ is a strong electrolyte. What will be the concentration of all the ions in a 0.9 M solution of ammonium phosphate?
    a. 0.9 M NH_4+, 0.9 M PO_4^{3-}
    b. 0.3 M NH_4+, 0.9 M PO_4^{3-}
    c. 2.7 M NH_4+, 0.9 M PO_4^{3-}
    d. 2.7 M NH_4^+, 2.7 M PO_4^{3-}

27. Which of the following represents the correct increasing order of acidity?
    a. $CH_3COOH < CH_3OH < CH_3CH_3 < HCl$
    b. $CH_3CH_3 < CH_3OH < CH_3COOH < HCl$
    c. $CH_3CH_3 < CH_3COOH < CH_3OH < HCl$
    d. $CH_3OH < CH_3CH_3 < HCl < CH_3COOH$

28. One liter of a 0.02 M solution of methanol in water is prepared. What is the mass of methanol in the solution, and what is the approximate molality of methanol?
    a. 0.64 g, 0.02 m
    b. 0.32 g, 0.01 m
    c. 0.64 g, 0.03 m
    d. 0.32 g, 0.02 m

29. A 1 M solution of NaCl (A) and a 0.5 M solution of NaCl (B) are joined together by a semi permeable membrane. What, if anything, is likely to happen between the two solutions?
    a. No change, the solvents and solutes are the same in each
    b. Water will migrate from A to B
    c. NaCl will migrate from A to B and water will migrate from B to A.
    d. Water will migrate from B to A.

30. Which of the following radioactive emissions results in an increase in atomic number?
    a. Alpha
    b. Beta
    c. Gamma
    d. Neutron

31. A material has a half life of 2 years. If you started with 1 kg of the material, how much would be left after 8 years?
    a. 1 kg
    b. 0.5 kg
    c. 0.06 kg
    d. 0.12 kg

32. C-14 has a half life of 5730 years. If you started with 1 mg of C-14 today, how much would be left in 20,000 years?
    a. 0.06 mg
    b. 0.07 mg
    c. 0.11 mg
    d. 0.09 mg

33. The best way to separate isotopes of the same element is to exploit:
    a. Differences in chemical reactivity
    b. Differences in reduction potential
    c. Differences in toxicity
    d. Differences in mass

34. Nuclear chain reactions, such as the one that is exploited in nuclear power plants, are propagated by what subatomic particle(s)?
    a. Protons
    b. Neutrons
    c. Electrons
    d. Neutrons and protons

35. Which of the following statements about radioactive decay is true?
    a. The sum of the mass of the daughter particles is less than that of the parent nucleus
    b. The sum of the mass of the daughter particles is greater than that of the parent nucleus
    c. The sum of the mass of the daughter particles is equal to that of the parent nucleus
    d. The sum of the mass of the daughter particles cannot be accurately measured

36. Determine the number of neutrons, protons and electrons in ^{238}U.
    a. 238, 92, 238
    b. 92, 146, 146
    c. 146, 92, 92
    d. 92, 92, 146

37. An alpha particle consists of
    a. Two electrons and two protons
    b. Two electrons and two neutrons
    c. Four neutrons
    d. Two protons and two neutrons

38. Describe the correct outer shell electronic arrangement of phosphorous.
    a. $4s^2\ 4p^3$
    b. $3s^2\ 3p^3$
    c. $2s^2\ 3p^3$
    d. $2s^2\ 2p^3$

39. Hund's rule regarding electronic configuration states:
    a. Electrons in the same orbital must have an opposite spin
    b. Electrons must fill lower energy orbitals before filling higher energy orbitals
    c. Electrons must populate empty orbitals of equal energy before filling occupied orbitals
    d. Electrons must have the same nuclear spin as the nucleus

40. Arrange the following elements in order of increasing atomic radius:
    a. K<Zn<Fe<As<Kr
    b. K<Fe<Zn<Kr<As
    c. Kr<As<Fe<K<Zn
    d. Kr<As<Zn<Fe<K

41. When a solid is heated and transforms directly to the gaseous phases, this process is called:
   a. sublimation
   b. fusion
   c. diffusion
   d. condensation

42. Determine the oxidation states of each of the elements in $KMnO_4$:
   a. K^{+1}, Mn^{+7}, O^{-8}
   b. K^{-1}, Mn^{+7}, O^{-2}
   c. K^{+1}, Mn^{+3}, O^{-4}
   d. K^{+1}, Mn^{+7}, O^{-2}

43. Place the following elements in order of decreasing electronegativity:
   N, As, Bi, P, Sb
   a. As>Bi>N>P>Sb
   b. N>P>As>Sb>Bi
   c. Bi>Sb>As>P>N
   d. P>N>As>Sb>Bi

44. Arrange the following compounds from most polar to least polar:
   F_2, CH_3CH_2Cl, NaCl, CH_3OH
   a. NaCl>CH_3OH> CH_3CH_2Cl> F_2
   b. F_2> NaCl> CH_3OH>CH_3CH_2Cl
   c. CH_3OH>NaCl>F_2>CH_3CH_2Cl
   d. NaCl>F_2>CH_3OH>CH_3CH_2Cl

45. Which of the following is an incorrect Lewis structure?

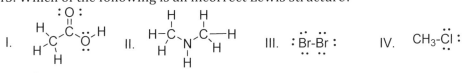

   a. I
   b. II
   c. III
   d. IV

46. Which bond has the shortest length?
   a. sp^2
   b. sp^3
   c. sp
   d. pi

47. Resonance structures can be defined as:
   a. Two or more structures that have different atoms bound to different atoms
   b. Two structures that have a similar structure but different formula
   c. Two or more structures that have the same formula, but are different in shape
   d. Two or more structures that differ only in the arrangement of electrons in the structures

48. Atoms that are sp^2 hybridized will have what sort of hybrid orbital geometry around them?
    a. Tetrahedral
    b. Trigonal planar
    c. Linear
    d. Angled

49. What is the chemical composition of ammonium sulfate?
    a. N 21%, H 3%, S 24%, O 32%
    b. N 10%, H 6%, S 24%, O 60%
    c. N 10%, H 4%, S 12%, O 74%
    d. N 21%, H 6%, S 24%, O 48%

50. What is the correct IUPAC name of the compound Fe_2O_3?
    a. Iron (I) oxide
    b. Iron (II) oxide
    c. Iron (III) oxide
    d. Iron (IV) oxide

51. Balance the following reaction between sulfuric acid and aluminum hydroxide by filling in the correct stoichiometric values for each chemical.
    $$\_\ H_2SO_4 + \_\ Al(OH)_3 \ \rightarrow \_\ Al_2(SO_4)_3 + \_\ H_2O$$
    a. 3, 2, 1, 6
    b. 2, 3, 1, 3
    c. 3, 3, 2, 6
    d. 1, 2, 1, 4

52. Calculate the mass of water produced from the reaction of 1 kg of n-heptane with oxygen.
    n-heptane (1 kg) + 11 O_2 $\rightarrow$ 7 CO_2 + 8 H_2O
    a. 144 g
    b. 8 kg
    c. 800 g
    d. 1.4 kg

53. Magnesium metal is reacted with hydrobromic acid according to the following equation:
    $$Mg + 2HBr \rightarrow MgBr_2 + H_2$$
    If 100 g of Mg is reacted with 100 g of HBr, which statement about the reaction is true?
    a. Mg is the limiting reagent
    b. HBr is the excess reagent
    c. Mg is the excess reagent
    d. 100 g of $MgBr_2$ will be produced

54. Methane gas is burned in pure oxygen at 200 °C and 1 atm of pressure to produce CO_2 and H_2O according to the equation

$$CH_4 + 2O_2 \rightarrow CO_2 + 2H_2O$$

If 10 L of methane gas were burned, and the final temperature and pressure remained the same, how many liters of gaseous products are produced by the reaction?
   a. 10 L
   b. 20 L
   c. 30 L
   d. 40 L

55. The overall reaction A→D can be described by the following equation:

$$A \xrightarrow{\text{fast}} B \xrightarrow{\text{slow}} C \xrightarrow{\text{fast}} D$$

What would be the rate law for the overall reaction of A to D?
   a. Rate = k[D]/[A]
   b. Rate = k[B]
   c. Rate = [B]
   d. Rate = k[C]/[B]

56. How many electrons are in the atom $_{20}^{45}Ca$?
   a. 20
   b. 45
   c. 65
   d. 25

57. For the reaction $CO_2(g) + H_2(g) \rightarrow CO(g) + H_2O(l)$, which of the following will occur if the pressure of the reaction is increased?
   a. The reaction rate will increase
   b. The reaction rate will decrease
   c. The reaction equilibrium will shift to the right
   d. The reaction equilibrium will shift to the left

58. For the gas phase reaction $CH_4 + 4Cl_2 \rightarrow CCl_4 + 4HCl$, what would be the equilibrium expression K_{eq} for this reaction?
   a. $[CH_4][Cl_2] / [CCl_4][4HCl]$
   b. $[CH_4][Cl_2] / [CCl_4][HCl]^4$
   c. $[4Cl][CCl_4}/[CH_4][4HCl]$
   d. $[CCl_4][HCl]^4/ [CH_4][Cl_2]^4$

59. Adding a catalyst to a reaction will do which of the following to that reaction:
   a. Shift the reaction equilibrium towards the products
   b. Increase the temperature of the reaction
   c. Decrease the energy of activation for the reaction
   d. Increase the purity of the reaction products

60. 10 g of salt XY (MW = 100 g/mol) is added to 1 liter of water with stirring. The salt dissociates into ions X^+ and Y^-. After equilibrium is established, the undissolved portion of the salt was removed by filtration, weighed, and found to be 9.5 g. What is the K_{sp} for this salt?

    a. 5×10^{-2}
    b. 5 x 10-3
    c. 1 x10-2
    d. 2.5×10^{-5}

61. Which of the following are considered Lewis acids?

    I. H_2SO_4
    II. $AlCl_3$
    III. PCl_3
    IV. $FeCl_3$

    a. II and IV
    b. II and III
    c. I and IV
    d. I and II

62. Place the following in the correct order of increasing acidity:

    H_3PO_4, HF, HCl, H_2O, NH_3

    a. $H_3PO4 < H_2O < NH_3 < HF < HCl$
    b. $NH_3 < H_2O < HF < H_3PO_4 < HCl$
    c. $H_2O < NH_3 < HF < H_3PO_4 < HCl$
    d. $NH_3 < H_2O < HF < HCl < H_3PO_4$

63. The pka for ethanol (CH_3CH_2OH) is approximately 16. The pka for acetic acid (CH_3COOH) is about 4. The difference can be explained by:

    a. Resonance stabilization
    b. Electronegativity differences
    c. Molecular weight differences
    d. Molecular size differences

64. What will be the pH of 2 L of a 0.1 M aqueous solution of HCl?

    a. 2
    b. -1
    c. 1
    d. 0.05

65. What is the pH of a buffer containing 0.2 M NaOAc and 0.1 M HOAc? The pka of acetic acid is 4.75.

    a. 4
    b. 5
    c. 6
    d. 7

66. 50 mL of 1 M H_2SO_4 is added to an aqueous solution containing 4 g of NaOH. What will the final pH of the resulting solution be?
   a. 5
   b. 6
   c. 7
   d. 9

67. To make a good buffering system in the pH range of 5-9, which acid/base combinations would likely work the best?
   a. HCl/NaOH
   b. HNO_3/$NaNO_3$
   c. H_2SO_4/$NaHSO_4$
   d. NaH_2PO_4/Na_2HPO_4

68. For the conversion of water into steam, which of the following is true?
   a. $\Delta T=0$, $\Delta S>0$
   b. $\Delta T>0$, $\Delta S = 0$
   c. $\Delta T =0$, $\Delta S <0$
   d. $\Delta T >0$, $\Delta S >0$

69. 100 g of NH_3 are cooled from 100 °C to 25 °C. What is the heat change for this transition? The heat capacity of ammonia gas is 35.1 J/(mol) (°K)
   a. -263KJ
   b. 15.5 KJ
   c. -15.5KJ
   d. 263 KJ

70. Determine the heat of combustion for the following reaction:
   Propane + 5 O_2 →3 CO_2 + 4 H_2O
   The standard heats of formation for propane, CO_2 and water are -103.8 KJ/mol, -393.5 KJ/mol and -285.8 KJ/mol respectively.
   a. -2220 KJ/mol
   b. -2323.7 kJ/mol
   c. 2220 KJ/mol
   d. 2323.7 KJ/mol

71. Which of the following reactions produces products with higher entropy than the starting materials?
   I. Glucose (s) + water →glucose (aq)
   II. 4Al (s) + 3O_2(g) →2Al_2O_3(s)
   III. Br_2 + light→2 Br
   IV. Ice →water vapor
   a. II, III
   b. I, II
   c. I, III
   d. I, III, IV

72. A 1kg block each of iron, lead and nickel are heated from 20 °C to 30 °C. Which of the following statements about the blocks is true?
    a. The lead will heat faster than the iron and the nickel.
    b. The iron required more heat to reach 30 °C than the nickel or lead.
    c. All three blocks required a different amount of heat to reach 30 °C.
    d. The iron required more time to reach 30 °C.

73. In the reaction $Pb + H_2SO_4 + H_2O \rightarrow PbSO_4 + H_2 + H_2O$
    a. Lead is reduced and hydrogen is oxidized
    b. Lead is oxidized and hydrogen is oxidized
    c. Lead is reduced and sulfate is oxidized
    d. Lead is oxidized and hydrogen is reduced

74. Which of the following elements would likely be good reducing agents?
    a. Br_2
    b. N_2
    c. Na
    d. Ne

75. Molten magnesium chloride is electrolyzed. The products formed from this reaction are:
    a. Mg(0) at the anode and Cl- at the cathode
    b. Mg2+ at the anode and Cl- at the cathode
    c. Mg (0) at the cathode and Cl_2 at the anode
    d. Mg(0) at the anode and Cl_2 at the cathode

76. The transformation of diamond to graphite has a $-\Delta G$. Which of the following is true?
    a. The reaction is spontaneous and occurs rapidly at room temperature
    b. The reaction is not spontaneous and occurs slowly at room temperature
    c. The reaction is not spontaneous and does not occur at room temperature
    d. The reaction is spontaneous and occurs slowly at room temperature

77. What would be the correct IUPAC name for the following compound?

    a. 3-methyl-2-butanol
    b. 2-methyl-3-butanol
    c. 3,3-dimethyl-2-propanol
    d. 2-Hydroxy-3-methyl butane

78. Which of the following molecules are alkenes?

I.

II.

III.

IV.

    a. I
    b. II
    c. III
    d. IV

79. What is the oxidation state of the carbon atom in a carboxylic acid functional group?
    a. 4+
    b. 3+
    c. 2-
    d. 3-

80. Which of the following molecules is named correctly?

A.

methyl propionoate

B.   OH

1-propanol

C.

3-propanoic acid

D.

3-butene

81. Which scientist was responsible for developing the modern periodic table?
    a. Faraday
    b. Einstein
    c. Hess
    d. Mendeleev

82. Two different molecules can be isomers of each other if:
    a. They have the same functional groups
    b. They have the same oxidation state
    c. They have the same molecular weight
    d. They have the same chemical formula

83. Which of the following molecules are cis alkenes?

I.   II.

III.   IV.

    a. I, II
    b. II, III
    c. III, IV
    d. I, IV

84. What would be the best analytical tool for determining the chemical structure of an organic compound?
    a. NMR
    b. HPLC
    c. IR
    d. Mass spec

85. Proteins are made up of which of the following repeating subunits?
    a. Sugars
    b. Triglycerides
    c. Amino acids
    d. Nucleic acids

86. The precision of a number of data points refers to:
    a. How accurate the data is
    b. How many errors the data contains
    c. How close the data points are to the mean of the data
    d. How close the actual data is to the predicted result

87. The density of a material refers to:
    a. Mass per volume
    b. Mass per mole
    c. Molecular weight per volume
    d. Moles per volume

88. Which of the following types of chemicals are considered generally unsafe to store together?
    I. Liquids and solids
    II. Acids and bases
    III. Reducing agents and oxidizing agents
    IV. Metals and salts
    a. I, II
    b. II, III
    c. III, IV
    d. I, IV

89. Which statement about the impact of chemistry on society is not true?
   a. Fluoridation of water has had no effect on the rate of cavities as compared to unfluoridated water
   b. Chemical fertilizers have tremendously increased food production per acre in the U.S.
   c. Chemistry played a central role in the development of nuclear weapons
   d. Use of catalytic converters in automobiles has greatly reduced acid rain producing exhaust products

90. Methyl mercury is a toxin produced indirectly from what energy source?
   a. Oil
   b. Natural gas
   c. Wood
   d. Coal

Multiple Choice Answers

1. B: Na (sodium) is a solid at standard temperature and pressure, which is 0°C (273 K) and 100 kPa (0.986 atm), according to IUPAC. The stronger the intermolecular forces, the greater the likelihood of the material being a solid. Kr and Xe are noble gases and have negligible intermolecular attraction. NH_3 has some hydrogen bonding but is still a gas at STP. Sodium is an alkali metal whose atoms are bonded by metallic bonding and is therefore a solid at STP.

2. D: Generally, the larger and heavier the molecule, the higher the melting point. Decreasing polarity will lower intermolecular attractions and lower the melting point. Long, linear molecules have a larger surface area, and therefore more opportunity to interact with other molecules, which increases the melting point.

3. A: The kinetic energy of the gas molecules is directly proportional to the temperature. If the temperature decreases, so does the molecular motion. A decrease in temperature will not necessarily mean a gas condenses to a liquid. Neither the mass nor the density is impacted, as no material was added or removed, and the volume remained the same.

4. B: The ideal gas law PV=nRT is rearranged to solve for V, and we get V = nRT/P. R is the gas constant, 0.08206 L atm/mol K, and the Celsius temperature must be converted to Kelvin, by adding 273 to 25°C to obtain 298 K. The pressure must be converted to atmospheres, which 101 kPa is essentially 1 atm (0.9967 atm). Plugging the numbers into the equation we get V = 1000 mol (0.08206 L atm/mol K)(298 K)/1 atm, which gives V = 24,453 L. A liter is a cubic decimeter (dm^3) and when converted gives V = 24.5 m^3.

5. D: Since there are twice as many molecules of hydrogen present vs. oxygen, the partial pressure of hydrogen will be greater. The mass of hydrogen will not be greater than the mass of oxygen present even though there are more moles of hydrogen, due to oxygen having a higher molecular weight. Each gas will occupy the same volume. Hydrogen and oxygen gas can coexist in the container without reacting to produce water. There is no indication given that a chemical reaction has occurred.

6. C: Graham's law of diffusion allows one to calculate the relative diffusion rate between two different gases based on their masses.

7. D: London dispersion forces are the weakest intermolecular forces. These interactions occur in all molecules due to unequal electron density around the nucleus, which results in a momentary dipole. Dipole-dipole interactions are those between two polar molecules. The more positive portion of one molecule is attracted to the negative portion of a different molecule. Hydrogen bonding is a stronger type of dipole-dipole interaction which occurs between a hydrogen in one molecule and a nitrogen, oxygen or fluorine atom in another molecule. Hydrogen bonding only occurs between molecules containing H-F, H-O or H-N

- 156 -

bonds. Ionic bonds are the strongest intermolecular forces. In ionic molecules, a positive ion is attracted to a negative ion. NaCl is entirely ionic with full charge separation, and the ions are tightly bound to each other in an organized crystalline network.

8. B: Plugging the data into the ideal gas law using the correct units gives the correct answer in atmospheres, which in this case is 2.4 atm. The equation is $P = nRT/V$. So we have P = 1 mol (0.08206 L atm/mol K)(298 K)/10 L. The R value is 0.08206 L atm/mol K when using L as the volume unit, and delivers the pressure in atm.

9. A: Since there are 7 moles of neon out of a total of 14 moles of gas in the cylinder, the partial pressure of neon will always be 50% of the total pressure, regardless of the temperature.

10. C: To convert from degrees Celsius to Kelvin, add 273. 75° C is equivalent to 348 K. Both X and Y have lower boiling points, which means that they will each boil in the water bath. Z will never become warm enough to boil.

11. D: Both liquids and gases are fluids and therefore flow, but only gases are compressible. The molecules that make up a gas are very far apart, allowing the gas to be compressed into a smaller volume.

12. C: The most electronegative atoms are found near the top right of the periodic table. Fluorine has a high electronegativity, while Francium, located at the bottom left on the table, has a low electrongativity.

13. B: Since both the volume and the temperature remain fixed, the only variable that changes is the number of moles of particles. Because there are now 3 times the number of particles as there were originally, the pressure must increase proportionately and so the pressure must be 3 atm.

14. C: As the temperature drops to -5 °C, the water vapor condenses to a liquid, and then to a solid. The vapor pressure of a solid is much less than that of the corresponding gas. The argon is still a gas at -5 °C, so almost all the pressure in the cylinder is due to argon.

15. A: Heat is absorbed by the solid during melting, therefore ΔH is positive. Going from a solid to a liquid greatly increases the freedom of the particles, therefore increasing the entropy, so ΔS is also positive.

16. B: Freezing is an exothermic event; therefore heat must be given off. The temperature of the material remains unchanged at the freezing point during the process.

17. A: The higher the temperature of the liquid, the greater the solubility of the solid, while the higher the temperature, the lower the solubility of the gas.

18. C: Normality refers to the concentration of acid equivalents (H^+ ions), not the concentration of the solute. 100 g of phosphoric acid has a MW of 98 g/mol. So, 100g/98 g/mol = 1.02 moles of phosphoric acid are in solution. The total volume of the solution is 0.4 L, so the molarity of the solution is 1.02 mol/0.4 L = 2.55 M. Since there are three acid equivalents for every mole of phosphoric acid, the normality is 3 x 2.55 = 7.65 N.

19. D: $AgNO_3$, $NaNO_3$ and NaCl are all highly water soluble and would not precipitate under these conditions. All nitrate compounds and compounds containing Group I metals are soluble in water. AgCl is essentially insoluble in water, and this is the precipitate observed.

20. B: Density is determined by dividing the mass of the solution by its volume. The mass is 200 g, and the total volume is 0.2 L, or 200 mL. So 200 g/200 mL = 1 g/mL.

21. D: 100 mL of a 0.1 M solution of NaOH contains 0.01 moles of NaOH. That means 0.01 moles of acid are required to completely neutralize the solution. The MW of sulfuric acid is 98, so 0.98 g of sulfuric acid is 0.01 mole. But since sulfuric acid has two equivalents of acid per mole, only 0.005 mole of the acid is required or 0.49 g.

22. B: Pure water boils at 100 °C. Water that has salts dissolved in it will boil at a slightly higher temperature, and will conduct electricity much better than pure water.

23. D: Acidity increases as we travel down the periodic table with regard to the halogens. Even though fluorine is the most electronegative element and would be expected to stabilize a negative charge well, it is such a small atom that it is poorly able to stabilize the negative charge and therefore will have a stronger bond to the hydrogen. As the atoms get larger, moving from fluorine to iodine, the ability to stabilize a negative charge becomes greater and the bond with the hydrogen is weaker. A stronger bond with the between the halogen and the hydrogen will result in less acidity, since fewer hydrogen ions will be produced.

24. D: Octane is a nonpolar hydrocarbon with little or no water solubility. Butanol is an alcohol with a small amount of solubility due to its polar –OH group. Ethanol is a smaller, more polar alcohol that is very soluble in water. NaCl is an ionic salt that is highly soluble in water.

25. A: The weight % of the acetic acid is the mass of acetic acid divided by the mass of the acetic acid plus the water. So 50g/(50g +200g) = 0.2, or 20%. The mole fraction is the moles of acetic acid divided by the total number of moles of the solution. So 50 g of acetic acid (MW = 60) is 50g/ 60 g/mol = 0.83 moles. 200 g of water = 11.11 moles. Therefore, 0.83 mol/(0.83 mol + 11.11 mol) = 0.069.

26. C: Since there are three moles of NH_4^+ per mole of salt and 1 mole of PO_4^{3-} per mole of salt, the total ionic concentrations must be 2.7 M of NH_4^+, and 0.9 M of PO_4^{3-}.

27. B: Ethane is an alkane and only very weakly acidic. Methanol, an alcohol, has a slightly acidic proton attached to the oxygen. Acetic acid is much more acidic than methanol with the acidic proton attached to the carboxyl group. Hydrochloric acid is highly acidic and completely dissociates in water.

28. A: Since we have 1 liter of the solution, then 0.02 M represents 0.02 moles of methanol. The mass of methanol can then be found by 0.02mol x MW of CH_3OH (32) = 0.64 g. Molality is the moles of solute (methanol) divided by the number of kilograms of solvent, in this case, it is essentially 1 kg. This is assumed since the solvent is water and the density of water is 1 g/mL. So 0.02 mol/ 1 kg = 0.02 m.

29. D: During osmosis, solvent flows from the lowest to the highest concentration of solute, in this case B to A. The membrane is semi-permeable and only allows the solvent to move, not the solute.

30. B: Beta emission represents the spontaneous decay of a neutron into a proton with the release of an electron. Therefore the resulting nucleus will have one more proton than it did before the reaction, and protons represent the atomic number of an atom. Alpha decay results in the emission of a helium nucleus. The resulting nucleus of an alpha decay would lose two protons and two neutrons, causing a decrease in both the atomic number and the mass number. Gamma decay does not affect the numbers of protons or neutrons in the nucleus. It is an emission of a photon, or packet of energy.

31. C: Since each half life is 2 years, eight years would be 4 half lives. So the mass of material is halved 4 times. Therefore if we start with 1 kg, at two years we would have 0.5 kg, at four years we would have 0.25 kg, after 6 years we would have 0.12 kg, and after 8 years we would have 0.06 kg.

32. D: Using the decay formula, C-14 remaining = C-14 initial$(0.5)^{t/t \text{ half-life}}$. So, 1 mg $(0.5)^{20000/5730}$ = 0.09 mg. This problem is best solved using the decay formula since 20,000 years is 3.5 half lives. If a student is careful in their reasoning, this problem can be solved without the decay formula. After 3 half-lives, there would be 0.125 mg remaining. If allowed to decay for 4 half-lives, 0.0625 mg would remain. Since only half of this half-life were allowed to elapse, only half of the material would decay, which would be 0.03 mg. Subtracting this amount from 0.125 mg, the amount remaining after 3 half-lives, gives 0.09 mg, which is the amount of material remaining after 3.5 half-lives.

33. D: Isotopes of the same element must have the same chemical behavior, so A, B, and C all represent, in one form or another, chemical behavior. Isotopes differ in mass, and this can be used to separate them by some appropriate physical property.

34. B: Neutrons are neutral in charge, and can impact a nucleus in order to break it.

35. A: Nuclear reactions convert mass into energy ($E = mc^2$). The mass of products is always less than that of the starting materials since some mass is now energy.

36. C: The mass number is the number of protons and the number of neutrons added together. The number of protons is also known as the atomic number and can be found on the periodic table. Therefore, the number of neutrons is the mass number (238) less the number of protons, in this case, 92, so we have 146 neutrons. The number of electrons always equals the number of protons in a neutral atom, so C is the correct answer.

37. D: An alpha particle is a helium nucleus, which contains two protons and two neutrons.

38. B: Phosphorus is in the third period, so the outermost levels must be 3s, 3p. Phosphorus is in Group 5A, which indicates that it has 5 valence electrons. To fill the 3s and 3p, 2 electrons first fill the s orbital, and then the remaining 3 electrons enter the p orbitals. So, $3s^2\ 3p^3$.

39. C: Hund's rule states that electrons must populate empty orbitals of similar energy before pairing up. The Aufbau principle states that electrons must fill lower energy orbitals before filling higher energy orbitals. The Pauli exclusion principle states that no two electrons in the same atom can have the same four quantum numbers, and therefore, two electrons in the same orbital will have opposite spins.

40. D: All of the elements belong to the same row in the periodic table. Atomic radii increase going from right to left in any row of the periodic table. Although these elements belonged to the same row, it is important to also know that atomic radii increase from top to bottom in the groups of the periodic table.

41. A: Sublimation is the process of a solid changing directly into a gas without entering the liquid phase. Fusion refers to a liquid turning into a solid. Diffusion is the process of a material dispersing throughout another. Condensation is generally a gas turning into a liquid.

42. D: Each oxygen has a charge of -2 for a total negative charge of -8. Potassium (K) only exists in compounds as +1. Therefore for the molecule to have a neutral charge, the Mn must be in a +7 oxidation state.

43. B: The trend within any column of the periodic table is that electronegativity decreases going down the column.

44. A: NaCl is an ionic salt, and therefore the most polar. F_2 is nonpolar since the two atoms share the electrons in an equal and symmetrical manner. CH_3OH is an alcohol with a very polar O-H bond. CH_3CH_2Cl is also a polar molecule due to the unequal sharing of electrons between in the C-Cl bond.

45. B: The nitrogen is missing its lone pair of electrons, and should have two dots above it. A correct Lewis structure shows how the atoms are connected to each other as well as all of the valence electrons in the compound. Each bond represents two electrons.

46. C: The more s character the bond has, the shorter it will be. A triple bond is stronger and shorter than a double bond, which is stronger and shorter than a single bond. An sp orbital is found in a triple bond. An sp^2 obital is found in a double bond and sp^3 orbitals are found in single bonds.

47. D: Resonance structures have the same atoms connected to the same atoms, but differ only in electronic structure amongst the atoms. Isomers are molecules that have the same formula but differ in structure. Structural isomers differ in how the atoms are bonded to each other. Stereoisomers are isomers that have the same bonding structure but different arrangements, for example, cis- and trans- isomers.

48. B: Hybrid orbitals arrange themselves to be as far from each other as possible. An sp^2 atom has three hybrid orbitals, so they arrange themselves to be trigonal planar, with 120 ° between the bonds.

49. D: The correct structure of ammonium sulfate is $(NH_4)_2SO_4$. Its molecular weight is 132. The masses of the elements in the compound are: nitrogen 28 (2 x 14), hydrogen 8 (1x8), sulfur 32 (32x1) and oxygen 64 (16x4). To find the percentage composition of each element, divide the element mass by the molecular weight of the compound and multiply by 100. So nitrogen is (28/132)x100 = 21%, hydrogen is (8/132)x100 = 6%, sulfur is (32/132)x100 = 24% and oxygen is (64/132)x100 = 48%.

50. C: Three oxygen are equal to a total charge of -6. Therefore, the two iron atoms must equal that with a positive charge, or +6. So each iron atom must be +3, and the compound is iron (III) oxide.

51. A: By comparing the products to the reactants, there must be at least two Al atoms in the starting material, and at least three sulfate groups. Therefore, a coefficient of 2 must be placed in front of $Al(OH)_3$ and a coefficient of 3 must be placed in front of H_2SO_4. To make the number of hydrogen and oxygen atoms equal on both sides of the equation, a coefficient of 6 must be placed in front of H_2O.

52. D: 1 kg of heptane (MW 100) is equal to 10 moles of heptane. Since 8 moles of water is produced for every mole of heptane reacted, 80 moles of water must be produced. 80 moles of water (MW 18) equals 1440 g, or 1.4 kg.

53. C: 100 g of HBr equals 1.23 moles, and 100 g of Mg equals 4.11 moles. From the coefficients of the balanced equation, the ratio of HBr to Mg is 2:1. This means that to react 1.23 moles of HBr, 2.46 moles of Mg would be required. Since 4.11 moles of Mg are present, Mg is in excess.

54. C: The equation shows that for every liter of methane reacted, one liter of CO_2 and 2 liters of water vapor will be produced. So a total of three liters of gaseous products will be formed for every liter of methane burned. Because the temperature of the reaction

products is 200 °C, the water produced will be in vapor (gas) form and not in liquid form. Since 10L of methane were burned, 30 L of gaseous products were formed.

55. B: Since the conversion of B to C is the slow step, this is the only one that determines the reaction rate law. Therefore, the rate law will be based on B, since it is the only reactant in producing C.

56. A: Since the atomic number is 20, which represents the number of protons in the atom, there must be an equal number of electrons in a neutral atom. Protons have a positive charge and electrons are negative. Equal numbers of protons and electrons will result in a neutral atom, or zero charge.

57. C: A pressure increase will force the reaction to go further to the right, which lowers gas pressure to restore equilibrium. Since the water formed is in the liquid phase, it does not appear in the equilibrium equation, so only 1 mole of gas is produced and is part of the equation.

58. D: For a general reaction, a A + b B→ c C + d D, the equilibrium equation would take the form:

$$K_{eq} = \frac{[C]^c [D]^d}{[A]^a [B]^b}$$

where a, b, c and d are the coefficients from the balanced chemical reaction. Pure liquids and solids are excluded from the equation. Since all reactants and products in the problem are gaseous, the equilibrium equation for the reaction would be:

$$K_{eq} = \frac{[CCl_4][HCl]^4}{[CH_4][Cl_2]^4}$$

59. C: Catalysts lower the energy barrier between products and reactants and thus increase the reaction rate.

60. D: 0.5 g of the salt dissolved, which is 0.005 mol of the salt. Since the volume is 1 L, the molarity of the salt is 0.005 M. This means that both species X and Y are present at 0.005 M concentration. The K_{sp} = [X][Y], or [0.005][0.005] which equals 2.5×10^{-5}.

61. A: Lewis acids are compounds capable of accepting a lone pair of electrons. $AlCl_3$ is a very strong Lewis acid and can readily accept a pair of electrons due to Al only having 6 electrons instead of 8 in its outer shell. $FeCl_3$ is also a strong Lewis acid, though milder than $AlCl_3$. Sulfuric acid is a Bronsted-Lowry acid since it produces protons. PCl_3 is a Lewis base since the P can donate its lone pair of electrons to another species.

62. B: NH_3 is ammonia, which is a base. H_2O is amphoteric, meaning that it can act as either a weak acid or a weak base. HF is actually a weak acid, despite fluorine being the most

- 162 -

electronegative atom. The small size of the F results in a stronger bond between the H and F, which reduces acidity since this bond will be harder to break. H_3PO_4, phosphoric acid, is high in acidity and HCl is a very strong acid, meaning it completely dissociates.

63. A: First, one must understand that pK_a is the acidity dissociation number. The larger the number, the less acidic. Acetic acid is a carboxylic acid. When H^+ is given off, a negative charge results on the O. Because there is a second equivalent oxygen bonded to the same carbon, this negative charge can be shared between both oxygen atoms. This is known as resonance stabilization and this conjugate base will be more stable and more of the acid molecules will remain dissociated resulting in higher acidity. For ethanol, when the O-H bond breaks, the negative charge resides completely on the O. It cannot be stabilized by other atoms and therefore reforms the methanol rapidly. This results in very low acidity, since very few protons will be released.

64. C: HCl is a strong acid that will completely dissociate. $pH = -\log_{10}[H^+]$, which for this problem is $pH = -\log_{10}(0.1) = 1$. The volume of the solution has no bearing on the pH since we know the concentration.

65. B: The K_a of acetic acid is determined from the pK_a, $K_a = 10^{-pka} = 1.75 \times 10^{-5}$. This is the equilibrium constant for the acetic acid dissociation, or $K_a = [H^+][CH_3COO^-]/[CH_3COOH]$. Using this equilibrium equation to solve for the $[H^+]$, the pH of the buffer can then be found. Solving for the $[H^+]$ concentration, we get $[H^+] = K_a \times [CH_3COOH]/CH_3COO^-]$, or $[H^+] = 1.75 \times 10^{-5} \times [0.1]/[0.2] = 8.75 \times 10^{-6}$. $pH = -\log[H^+] = 5.05$.

66. C: There are 0.05 mol of sulfuric acid being added, but a total of 0.10 mol of H^+ since sulfuric acid is diprotic (H_2SO_4). This is being added to 0.1 mol of NaOH. The moles of acid and base exactly cancel each other out; therefore the pH of the resulting aqueous solution will be near 7.

67. D: To make a buffer, a weak acid and its conjugate base or a weak base and its conjugate acid are commonly used. Buffers work by using the common-ion effect and result in little change in the pH when an acid or a base is added. HCl/NaOH is a strong acid/strong base combination and will not result in a buffer solution. Although the $HNO_3/NaNO_3$ and $H_2SO_4/NaHSO_4$ mixtures are conjugate acid/base pairs, both HNO_3 and H_2SO_4 are strong acids, not weak acids. Neither of these solutions would result in a buffer. Only the NaH_2PO_4/Na_2HPO_4 mixture would result in a buffer as it is a combination of a weak acid and its conjugate base.

68. A: When liquid water changes to steam, the temperature is constant, as in all phase changes. The entropy increases due to the increase in disorder from a liquid to a gas.

69. C: Cooling means heat is leaving the system, so it must be negative. We have 5.9 mol of ammonia cooling 75 °C, or 75 K. So 5.9 mol x -75 K x 35.1 J/(mol)(K) = -15.5 kJ.

70. A: The heat of combustion is determined by subtracting the heats of formation of the reactants from that of the products. So $3(-393.5) + 4(285.8) - (103.8) = -2220$.

71. D: In I, dissolving a solid into a liquid breaks up the organized solid matrix, therefore increasing disorder. III converts single particles into two particles, and in IV, solid ice sublimes into a gas. Both of these processes also increase disorder and thus, entropy. II is a decrease in entropy, since 7 molecules, with 3 being gaseous, are reacted to form 2 solid molecules.

72. C: Because all unique materials have differing heat capacities, no two can heat up the same way. All will require different amounts of heat to warm to the same temperature.

73. D: Lead (Pb) goes from a zero oxidation state to a 2+ oxidation state, and is therefore oxidized. Oxidation is the loss of electrons. Hydrogen goes from a 1+ oxidation state to a 0 oxidation state, and is therefore reduced. Reduction is the gaining of electrons.

74. C: Reducing agents give up electrons to another chemical species, which cause that species to gain an electron and become reduced. Oxidizing agents cause another species to be oxidized, or to lose an electron, and are themselves reduced as they gain that electron. Bromine is very electronegative, and is almost always an oxidizing agent. N_2 is nearly inert, or unreactive. Neon is an inert noble gas and would not be a reducing agent. Sodium (Na) is very reactive and eager to give up an electron, and is therefore a good reducing agent in a wide variety of reactions.

75. C: Reduction takes place at the cathode and oxidation takes place at the anode. Mg^{2+} of the salt will be reduced to $Mg(0)$ at the cathode, and Cl^- will be oxidized to Cl_2 at the anode.

76. D: The fact that ΔG for the reaction is negative indicates the reaction is spontaneous. This does not mean the reaction will be faster or slow. Diamonds as we all know do not rapidly convert to graphite, and in fact do so only very slowly, over millions of years, thank goodness.

77. A: The longest straight chain of carbons is four, so the parent name is butane. The alcohol takes number precedence, so it is in the -2- position, placing the methyl in the -3-position. The suffix becomes –ol since it is an alcohol, so the name is 3-methyl-2-butanol.

78. C: The first is an alkyne, which contains a triple bond between carbon atoms. The second is a ketone and contains a carbon-oxygen double bond. The third is an alkene, which has a double bond between two carbon atoms. The fourth is an imide, which contains a double bond between two nitrogen atoms.

79. B: The carbon of a carboxylic acid has three bonds to oxygen atoms and one to a carbon atom. The carbon bonded to the carboxylic carbon will have an oxidation state of zero. Each oxygen atom will have an oxidation number of -2. However, one oxygen is bonded to a hydrogen, which will have an oxidation number of +1. This results in a total oxidation

state of -3 for both oxygens bonded to the carbon. Therefore, since the carbon must balance the oxidation states of the oxygens (-3) and the carbon (0), the oxidation state of the carbon must be +3. The three bonds to oxygen give a +3, and the bond to carbon is 0.

80. A: B is 1-butanol, since its longest chain of carbons is 4, not 3. C is 3-pentanone, since there are 5 carbons in the chain and it is a ketone, rather than a carboxylic acid. D is 1-butene, not 3-butene. The name should be assigned by giving the double bond the lowest number.

81. D: Mendeleev was able to connect the trends of the different elements behaviors and develop a table that showed the periodicity of the elements and their relationship to each other.

82. D: Different molecules must have the same chemical formula to be isomers. They differ only in which atoms are bound to which. Having the same molecular weight does not necessarily mean two molecules have the same formula.

83. B: Cis isomers have substituent groups that are on the same side of the molecule across the double bond. Trans isomers are those with substituent groups that are on opposite sides of the molecule across the double bond. I is neither cis nor trans, since both substituents on the same carbon are identical. IV is trans because the two methyl groups are on opposite sides of the molecule. II is cis due to both ethyl groups being on the same side of the molecule. III is also considered cis, although each substituent is different. The heaviest groups on each end of the double bond must be on the same side of the double bond to be cis.

84. A: NMR, or nuclear magnetic resonance, allows one to determine the connectivity of atoms in an organic molecule, by "reading" the resonance signals from the attached hydrogen atoms. IR, or infrared spectroscopy, can help to identify the functional groups that are present, but does not give much information about its position in the molecule. Mass spectrometry breaks apart a large molecule and analyzes the masses of the fragments. It can be useful in analyzing protein structure. HPLC, or high performance liquid chromatography, is a method used to separate a mixture into its components.

85. C: Proteins are large polypeptides, comprised of many amino acids linked together by an amide bond. DNA and RNA are made up of nucleic acids. Carbohydrates are long chains of sugars. Triglycerides are fats and are composed of a glycerol molecule and three fatty acids.

86. C: The closer the data points are to each other, the more precise the data. This does not mean the data is accurate, but that the results are very reproducible.

87. A: Density is mass per volume, typically expressed in units such as g/cm^3, or kg/m^3.

88. B: Acids and bases will react violently if accidentally mixed, as will reducing and oxidizing agents. Both reactions can be highly exothermic and uncontrollable.

89. A: Communities around the world who drink fluoridated water have shown dramatic decreases in the number of dental cavities formed per citizen versus those communities that do not drink fluoridated water.

90. D: Combustion of coal releases significant amounts of Hg into the atmosphere. When the Hg settles into the water, it becomes methylated and concentrates in fish, making them toxic to eat.

Constructed Response

Platinum is a transition metal with atomic number 78. It is a member of group 10 and period 6 in the periodic table of elements. Platinum has a covalent radius of 136+/- 5pm. Applying your knowledge of the periodic table of elements and its organization, prepare a response in which you:

- Describe some of the common properties of elements in group 10 of the periodic table.

- List some of the other elements in group 10 and their properties.

- Discuss whether you would expect some of the elements in period 6 to have similar properties to platinum, and why or why not.

- Discuss the position and layout of transition metals within the periodic table.

- Explain what you can predict about the covalent radius of element numbers 77 and 79.

Secret Key #1 – Time is Your Greatest Enemy

To succeed on the TExES, you must use your time wisely.

Pace Yourself

Wear a watch. At the beginning of the test, check the time (or start a chronometer on your watch to count the minutes), and check the time after every few questions to make sure you are "on schedule."

If you are forced to speed up, do it efficiently. Usually one or more answer choices can be eliminated without too much difficulty. Above all, don't panic. Don't speed up and just begin guessing at random choices. By pacing yourself, and continually monitoring your progress against your watch, you will always know exactly how far ahead or behind you are with your available time. If you find that you are one minute behind on the test, don't skip one question without spending any time on it, just to catch back up. Take 15 fewer seconds on the next four questions, and after four questions you'll have caught back up. Once you catch back up, you can continue working each problem at your normal pace.

Furthermore, don't dwell on the problems that you were rushed on. If a problem was taking up too much time and you made a hurried guess, it must be difficult. The difficult questions are the ones you are most likely to miss anyway, so it isn't a big loss. It is better to end with more time than you need than to run out of time.

Lastly, sometimes it is beneficial to slow down if you are constantly getting ahead of time. You are always more likely to catch a careless mistake by working more slowly than quickly, and among very high-scoring test takers (those who are likely to have lots of time left over), careless errors affect the score more than mastery of material.

Secret Key #2 - Guessing is not Guesswork

You probably know that guessing is a good idea - unlike other standardized tests, there is no penalty for getting a wrong answer. Even if you have no idea about a question, you still have a 20-25% chance of getting it right.

Most test takers do not understand the impact that proper guessing can have on their score. Unless you score extremely high, guessing will significantly contribute to your final score.

Monkeys Take the Test

What most test takers don't realize is that to insure that 20-25% chance, you have to guess randomly. If you put 20 monkeys in a room to take this test, assuming they answered once per question and behaved themselves, on average they would get 20-25% of the questions correct. Put 20 test takers in the room, and the average will be much lower among guessed questions. Why?

1. The test writers intentionally writes deceptive answer choices that "look" right. A test taker has no idea about a question, so picks the "best looking" answer, which is often wrong. The monkey has no idea what looks good and what doesn't, so will consistently be lucky about 20-25% of the time.

2. Test takers will eliminate answer choices from the guessing pool based on a hunch or [...]ut correct answers often get excluded, leaving a 0% chance of [...] monkey has no clue, and often gets lucky with the best choice.

[...]elimination endorsed by most test courses is flawed and [...]nance- test takers don't guess, they make an ignorant stab in the [...]han random.

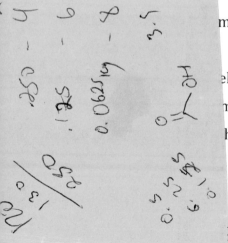

$5 Challenge

Let me introduce one of the most valuable ideas of this course- the $5 challenge:

You only mark your "best guess" if you are willing to bet $5 on it.
You only eliminate choices from guessing if you are willing to bet $5 on it.

Why $5? Five dollars is an amount of money that is small yet not insignificant, and can really add up fast (20 questions could cost you $100). Likewise, each answer choice on one question of the test will have a small impact on your overall score, but it can really add up to a lot of points in the end.

The process of elimination IS valuable. The following shows your chance of guessing it right:

If you eliminate wrong answer choices until only this many remain:	1	2	3
Chance of getting it correct:	100%	50%	33%

However, if you accidentally eliminate the right answer or go on a hunch for an incorrect answer, your chances drop dramatically: to 0%. By guessing among all the answer choices, you are GUARANTEED to have a shot at the right answer.

That's why the $5 test is so valuable- if you give up the advantage and safety of a pure guess, it had better be worth the risk.

What we still haven't covered is how to be sure that whatever guess you make is truly random. Here's the easiest way:

Always pick the first answer choice among those remaining.

Such a technique means that you have decided, **before you see a single test question**, exactly how you are going to guess- and since the order of choices tells you nothing about which one is correct, this guessing technique is perfectly random.

This section is not meant to scare you away from making educated guesses or eliminating choices- you just need to define when a choice is worth eliminating. The $5 test, along with a pre-defined random guessing strategy, is the best way to make sure you reap all of the benefits of guessing.

Secret Key #3 - Practice Smarter, Not Harder

Many test takers delay the test preparation process because they dread the awful amounts of practice time they think necessary to succeed on the test. We have refined an effective method that will take you only a fraction of the time.

There are a number of "obstacles" in your way to succeed. Among these are answering questions, finishing in time, and mastering test-taking strategies. All must be executed on the day of the test at peak performance, or your score will suffer. The test is a mental marathon that has a large impact on your future.

Just like a marathon runner, it is important to work your way up to the full challenge. So first you just worry about questions, and then time, and finally strategy:

Success Strategy

1. Find a good source for practice tests.
2. If you are willing to make a larger time investment, consider using more than one study guide- often the different approaches of multiple authors will help you "get" difficult concepts.
3. Take a practice test with no time constraints, with all study helps "open book." Take

your time with questions and focus on applying strategies.

4. Take a practice test with time constraints, with all guides "open book."

5. Take a final practice test with no open material and time limits

If you have time to take more practice tests, just repeat step 5. By gradually exposing yourself to the full rigors of the test environment, you will condition your mind to the stress of test day and maximize your success.

Secret Key #4 - Prepare, Don't Procrastinate

Let me state an obvious fact: if you take the test three times, you will get three different scores. This is due to the way you feel on test day, the level of preparedness you have, and, despite the test writers' claims to the contrary, some tests WILL be easier for you than others.

Since your future depends so much on your score, you should maximize your chances of success. In order to maximize the likelihood of success, you've got to prepare in advance. This means taking practice tests and spending time learning the information and test taking strategies you will need to succeed.

Never take the test as a "practice" test, expecting that you can just take it again if you need to. Feel free to take sample tests on your own, but when you go to take the official test, be prepared, be focused, and do your best the first time!

Secret Key #5 - Test Yourself

Everyone knows that time is money. There is no need to spend too much of your time or too little of your time preparing for the test. You should only spend as much of your precious time preparing as is necessary for you to get the score you need.

Once you have taken a practice test under real conditions of time constraints, then you will know if you are ready for the test or not.

If you have scored extremely high the first time that you take the practice test, then there is not much point in spending countless hours studying. You are already there.

Benchmark your abilities by retaking practice tests and seeing how much you have improved. Once you score high enough to guarantee success, then you are ready.

If you have scored well below where you need, then knuckle down and begin studying in earnest. Check your improvement regularly through the use of practice tests under real conditions. Above all, don't worry, panic, or give up. The key is perseverance!

Then, when you go to take the test, remain confident and remember how well you did on the practice tests. If you can score high enough on a practice test, then you can do the same on the real thing.

General Strategies

The most important thing you can do is to ignore your fears and jump into the test immediately- do not be overwhelmed by any strange-sounding terms. You have to jump into the test like jumping into a pool- all at once is the easiest way.

Make Predictions

As you read and understand the question, try to guess what the answer will be. Remember that several of the answer choices are wrong, and once you begin reading them, your mind will immediately become cluttered with answer choices designed to throw you off. Your mind is typically the most focused immediately after you have read the question and digested its contents. If you can, try to predict what the correct answer will be. You may be surprised at what you can predict.

Quickly scan the choices and see if your prediction is in the listed answer choices. If it is, then you can be quite confident that you have the right answer. It still won't hurt to check the other answer choices, but most of the time, you've got it!

Answer the Question

It may seem obvious to only pick answer choices that answer the question, but the test writers can create some excellent answer choices that are wrong. Don't pick an answer just because it sounds right, or you believe it to be true. It MUST answer the question. Once you've made your selection, always go back and check it against the question and make sure that you didn't misread the question, and the answer choice does answer the question posed.

Benchmark

After you read the first answer choice, decide if you think it sounds correct or not. If it doesn't, move on to the next answer choice. If it does, mentally mark that answer choice. This doesn't mean that you've definitely selected it as your answer choice, it just means that it's the best you've seen thus far. Go ahead and read the next choice. If the next choice is worse than the one you've already selected, keep going to the next answer choice. If the next choice is better than the choice you've already selected, mentally mark the new answer choice as your best guess.

The first answer choice that you select becomes your standard. Every other answer choice must be benchmarked against that standard. That choice is correct until proven otherwise by another answer choice beating it out. Once you've decided that no other answer choice seems as good, do one final check to ensure that your answer choice answers the question posed.

Valid Information

Don't discount any of the information provided in the question. Every piece of information may be necessary to determine the correct answer. None of the information in the question is there to throw you off (while the answer choices will certainly have information to throw you off). If two seemingly unrelated topics are discussed, don't ignore either. You can be confident there is a relationship, or it wouldn't be included in the question, and you are probably going to have to determine what is that relationship to find the answer.

Avoid "Fact Traps"

Don't get distracted by a choice that is factually true. Your search is for the answer that answers the question. Stay focused and don't fall for an answer that is true but incorrect. Always go back to the question and make sure you're choosing an answer that actually answers the question and is not just a true statement. An answer can be factually correct, but it MUST answer the question asked. Additionally, two answers can both be seemingly correct, so be sure to read all of the answer choices, and make sure that you get the one that BEST answers the question.

Milk the Question

Some of the questions may throw you completely off. They might deal with a subject you have not been exposed to, or one that you haven't reviewed in years. While your lack of knowledge about the subject will be a hindrance, the question itself can give you many clues that will help you find the correct answer. Read the question carefully and look for clues. Watch particularly for adjectives and nouns describing difficult terms or words that you don't recognize. Regardless of if you completely understand a word or not, replacing it with a synonym either provided or one you more familiar with may help you to understand what the questions are asking. Rather than wracking your mind about specific detailed

- 175 -

information concerning a difficult term or word, try to use mental substitutes that are easier to understand.

The Trap of Familiarity

Don't just choose a word because you recognize it. On difficult questions, you may not recognize a number of words in the answer choices. The test writers don't put "make-believe" words on the test; so don't think that just because you only recognize all the words in one answer choice means that answer choice must be correct. If you only recognize words in one answer choice, then focus on that one. Is it correct? Try your best to determine if it is correct. If it is, that is great, but if it doesn't, eliminate it. Each word and answer choice you eliminate increases your chances of getting the question correct, even if you then have to guess among the unfamiliar choices.

Eliminate Answers

Eliminate choices as soon as you realize they are wrong. But be careful! Make sure you consider all of the possible answer choices. Just because one appears right, doesn't mean that the next one won't be even better! The test writers will usually put more than one good answer choice for every question, so read all of them. Don't worry if you are stuck between two that seem right. By getting down to just two remaining possible choices, your odds are now 50/50. Rather than wasting too much time, play the odds. You are guessing, but guessing wisely, because you've been able to knock out some of the answer choices that you know are wrong. If you are eliminating choices and realize that the last answer choice you are left with is also obviously wrong, don't panic. Start over and consider each choice again. There may easily be something that you missed the first time and will realize on the second pass.

Tough Questions

If you are stumped on a problem or it appears too hard or too difficult, don't waste time. Move on! Remember though, if you can quickly check for obviously incorrect answer choices, your chances of guessing correctly are greatly improved. Before you completely give up, at least try to knock out a couple of possible answers. Eliminate what you can and then guess at the remaining answer choices before moving on.

Brainstorm

If you get stuck on a difficult question, spend a few seconds quickly brainstorming. Run through the complete list of possible answer choices. Look at each choice and ask yourself, "Could this answer the question satisfactorily?" Go through each answer choice and consider it independently of the other. By systematically going through all possibilities, you may find something that you would otherwise overlook. Remember that when you get stuck, it's important to try to keep moving.

Read Carefully

Understand the problem. Read the question and answer choices carefully. Don't miss the question because you misread the terms. You have plenty of time to read each question thoroughly and make sure you understand what is being asked. Yet a happy medium must be attained, so don't waste too much time. You must read carefully, but efficiently.

Face Value

When in doubt, use common sense. Always accept the situation in the problem at face value. Don't read too much into it. These problems will not require you to make huge leaps of logic. The test writers aren't trying to throw you off with a cheap trick. If you have to go beyond creativity and make a leap of logic in order to have an answer choice answer the question, then you should look at the other answer choices. Don't overcomplicate the problem by creating theoretical relationships or explanations that will warp time or space. These are normal problems rooted in reality. It's just that the applicable relationship or explanation may not be readily apparent and you have to figure things out. Use your common sense to interpret anything that isn't clear.

Prefixes

If you're having trouble with a word in the question or answer choices, try dissecting it. Take advantage of every clue that the word might include. Prefixes and suffixes can be a huge help. Usually they allow you to determine a basic meaning. Pre- means before, post-means after, pro - is positive, de- is negative. From these prefixes and suffixes, you can get an idea of the general meaning of the word and try to put it into context. Beware though of any traps. Just because con is the opposite of pro, doesn't necessarily mean congress is the opposite of progress!

Hedge Phrases

Watch out for critical "hedge" phrases, such as likely, may, can, will often, sometimes, often, almost, mostly, usually, generally, rarely, sometimes. Question writers insert these hedge phrases to cover every possibility. Often an answer choice will be wrong simply because it leaves no room for exception. Avoid answer choices that have definitive words like "exactly," and "always".

Switchback Words

Stay alert for "switchbacks". These are the words and phrases frequently used to alert you to shifts in thought. The most common switchback word is "but". Others include although, however, nevertheless, on the other hand, even though, while, in spite of, despite, regardless of.

New Information

Correct answer choices will rarely have completely new information included. Answer choices typically are straightforward reflections of the material asked about and will directly relate to the question. If a new piece of information is included in an answer choice that doesn't even seem to relate to the topic being asked about, then that answer choice is likely incorrect. All of the information needed to answer the question is usually provided for you, and so you should not have to make guesses that are unsupported or choose answer choices that require unknown information that cannot be reasoned on its own.

Time Management

On technical questions, don't get lost on the technical terms. Don't spend too much time on any one question. If you don't know what a term means, then since you don't have a dictionary, odds are you aren't going to get much further. You should immediately recognize terms as whether or not you know them. If you don't, work with the other clues that you have, the other answer choices and terms provided, but don't waste too much time trying to figure out a difficult term.

Contextual Clues

Look for contextual clues. An answer can be right but not correct. The contextual clues will help you find the answer that is most right and is correct. Understand the context in which a phrase or statement is made. This will help you make important distinctions.

Don't Panic

Panicking will not answer any questions for you. Therefore, it isn't helpful. When you first see the question, if your mind goes blank, take a deep breath. Force yourself to mechanically go through the steps of solving the problem and using the strategies you've learned.

Pace Yourself

Don't get clock fever. It's easy to be overwhelmed when you're looking at a page full of questions, your mind is full of random thoughts and feeling confused, and the clock is ticking down faster than you would like. Calm down and maintain the pace that you have set for yourself. As long as you are on track by monitoring your pace, you are guaranteed to have enough time for yourself. When you get to the last few minutes of the test, it may seem like you won't have enough time left, but if you only have as many questions as you should have left at that point, then you're right on track!

Answer Selection

The best way to pick an answer choice is to eliminate all of those that are wrong, until only one is left and confirm that is the correct answer. Sometimes though, an answer choice may immediately look right. Be careful! Take a second to make sure that the other choices are not equally obvious. Don't make a hasty mistake. There are only two times that you should stop before checking other answers. First is when you are positive that the answer choice you have selected is correct. Second is when time is almost out and you have to make a quick guess!

Check Your Work

Since you will probably not know every term listed and the answer to every question, it is important that you get credit for the ones that you do know. Don't miss any questions through careless mistakes. If at all possible, try to take a second to look back over your answer selection and make sure you've selected the correct answer choice and haven't made a costly careless mistake (such as marking an answer choice that you didn't mean to mark). This quick double check should more than pay for itself in caught mistakes for the time it costs.

Beware of Directly Quoted Answers

Sometimes an answer choice will repeat word for word a portion of the question or reference section. However, beware of such exact duplication – it may be a trap! More than likely, the correct choice will paraphrase or summarize a point, rather than being exactly the same wording.

Slang

Scientific sounding answers are better than slang ones. An answer choice that begins "To compare the outcomes…" is much more likely to be correct than one that begins "Because some people insisted…"

Extreme Statements

Avoid wild answers that throw out highly controversial ideas that are proclaimed as established fact. An answer choice that states the "process should be used in certain situations, if…" is much more likely to be correct than one that states the "process should be discontinued completely." The first is a calm rational statement and doesn't even make a definitive, uncompromising stance, using a hedge word "if" to provide wiggle room, whereas the second choice is a radical idea and far more extreme.

Answer Choice Families

When you have two or more answer choices that are direct opposites or parallels, one of them is usually the correct answer. For instance, if one answer choice states "x increases" and another answer choice states "x decreases" or "y increases," then those two or three answer choices are very similar in construction and fall into the same family of answer choices. A family of answer choices is when two or three answer choices are very similar in construction, and yet often have a directly opposite meaning. Usually the correct answer choice will be in that family of answer choices. The "odd man out" or answer choice that doesn't seem to fit the parallel construction of the other answer choices is more likely to be incorrect.

Special Report: Additional Bonus Material

Due to our efforts to try to keep this book to a manageable length, we've created a link that will give you access to all of your additional bonus material.

Please visit http://www.mometrix.com/bonus948/texeschem7-12 to access the information.